Design Process Hand-Sketching for Interiors

Rick Bartholomew

ISBN: 978-1-58503-825-1

Publications

Schroff Development Corporation

www.SDCpublications.com

Schroff Development Corporation
P.O. Box 1334
Mission KS 66222
(913) 262-2664
www.SDCpublications.com

Publisher: Stephen Schroff

Table of Contents

Acknowledgements

My parents, Helen and Leroy, who throughout my adolescent years in Pennsylvania nurtured a passion within for drawing and design and gave me the opportunity and funds to attend college at Oklahoma State University. The university experience in architectural design school and a graduate program in interior design gave me a phenomenal variety of hand-drawn visual exploration techniques to build upon my skills to take with me into professional practice after graduation. I wish to recognize professors Chris and Cuth Salmon, Kay Stewart, Margaret Weber, and Lynn Sisler who fostered my design and visual illustration skills while pursuing my degrees.

During my professional career, the firms and individuals I worked for and with gave me opportunities to enhance these skills; especially Arthur Johnson, Roseanne Bell, Kinslow, Keith, and Todd, Inc., all Tulsa designers and architects. A sincere thank you goes to June Gilliam of Stillwater, Oklahoma for her professional friendship of over 25 years in our collaborative work. Her design expertise and inspiration were significant factors in my drawing, sketching, and color rendering capabilities and development. I wish to thank my clients for your approvals to use the sketches that I created for them during the course of my professional career.

My students have always been a source of inspiration and motivation to sustain a renewing level of instruction insight for their needs in their development of hand-sketching techniques and various types of visual illustrations. It is so gratifying to see students succeed and surpass in their technique and say, "yes, I can do this." Through the classes I teach and the workshops I conduct around the country are enthusiastically supported by the interior design program here at Oklahoma State University, and this has spurred my passion for hand-sketching and rendering illustrations. A "colleague" thank you goes to Melinda Lyon at OSU for notifying me of this publication opportunity.

We all have people in our lives that are always there for support and encouragement of one's creative work, and they are friends and family. A special thank you to Doug Guss, my partner and friend for always being there for me! Your encouragement and support of my creative endeavors over the years I will always cherish.

About the Author

Rick Bartholomew is a Registered Oklahoma Interior Designer with thirty-five years of practicum experience in residential, commercial, and furniture design. He has a Bachelor of Architecture and Master of Science (Interior Design) degrees from Oklahoma State University, of which, he is currently a professor teaching in the Interior Design program in the Department of Design, Housing, and Merchandising. Professor Bartholomew was tenured at OSU during his seventeen years of teaching experience. His area of specialization is furniture design and presentation techniques. He has designed furniture pieces for exhibition and gallery showrooms in Oklahoma, Arizona, New Mexico, New York, Houston, and Chicago in addition to ownership of a copyrighted furniture collection inspired by Native American history and culture. Rick was a design consultant for a national retail fixture and custom furnishings manufacturer and his current work includes working with design and furniture manufacturing firms in developing furnishings and furniture components, as well as conducting sketching and color rendering workshops across the country.

Rick's passion, in addition to furnishings design, is dedicated to teaching students and practitioners the art and necessity of hand-sketching techniques and color marker and watercolor rendering illustrations. He also strives to foster the importance of quality visual presentation composition and information graphics. His is personally inspired by Native American history and culture, the work of Frank Lloyd Wright, Georgia O'Keeffe, Nicolai Fechin, Art Deco, and contemporary design.

**Author's Note**: **All sketches in the book are represented by a number in the "shaded" gray box near each illustration as recognition to the author's clients for their approval to use the sketches and/or their derivatives created for them for this publication.**

All other illustrations/sketches (not numbered are the sole ownership/designs of the author.

Preface

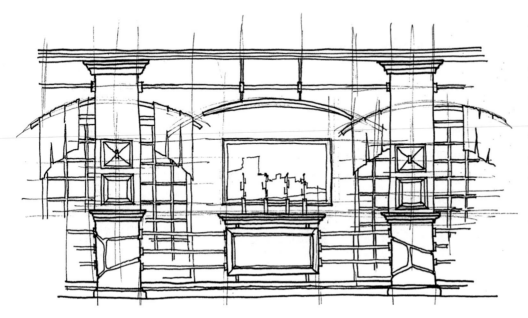

It is the intent of this book to develop hand-sketching skills that students can develop to enhance their basic knowledge of drawing techniques to use throughout the educational "design process." A review of basic drawing types is discussed in Ideation Chapters 2 through 4. The text is also intended to be a visual resource to aid the design student in visual presentation technique enhancements for various types of illustrations needed to portray their concepts. The practice of hand-sketched concept presentations is still viewed as important *design process* building blocks prior to final CAD-generated documents.

One course in hand drafting and/or sketching is not enough experience for the student learner; it must be fostered development and practice in subsequent coursework that enhances the design process. Hand-sketching techniques for plans, elevations, sections, various 3-dimensional illustrations, millwork and construction details are covered in the book in addition to an important issue of initial design processes of bubble diagramming, block and space plans. Information graphics, delineations, and visual composition are also topics addressed to enhance the visual communication of preliminary design concepts. Ideation Chapter 10 is a series of copyright-free line drawings to explore your skill building through practice exercises referred to within each chapter. I hope the book will be a valuable resource for each student's educational career as well as a refresher from time-to-time during your professional endeavors.

Reinforcing the components of the design process through hand-sketching skills and technique is regaining prominence within the educational experiences of future designers and the professional working environment as a means of validating creative concept thinking. The educational intent of this book can be visually summarized in the graphic illustration below to generate the various topic discussions to follow in assisting the student designer to develop their comfortable level of hand-sketched process drawings.

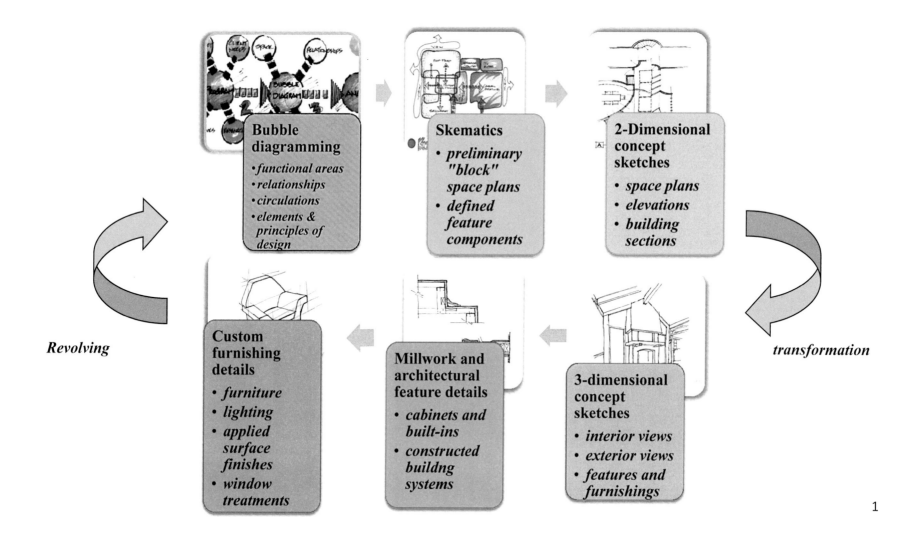

Bubble diagramming
- *functional areas*
- *relationships*
- *circulations*
- *elements & principles of design*

Skematics
- *preliminary "block" space plans*
- *defined feature components*

2-Dimensional concept sketches
- *space plans*
- *elevations*
- *building sections*

Custom furnishing details
- *furniture*
- *lighting*
- *applied surface finishes*
- *window treatments*

Millwork and architectural feature details
- *cabinets and built-ins*
- *constructed buildng systems*

3-dimensional concept sketches
- *interior views*
- *exterior views*
- *features and furnishings*

Revolving

transformation

1

Webster's New World Dictionary and Thesaurus (2nd Edition) defines **metamorphosis** as: "a change of form, structure, substance, or function; the ability to transform." As a designer begins the process of satisfying a project's requirements and needs, conveying this information visually is a *transformation of ideas/concepts*. Depending on project requirement demands, the process could start and/or stop at any step throughout the revolving transformation of the various components of the design concept(s), but inter-related among those components. *Your* design process, using the graphic chart on the previous page, is a reminder of the ever-changing drawing process. Or, the graphic chart could lead the student designer through every phase of the graphic chart. *It is important to first understand the requested intent for the type(s) of sketches needed by the viewer or audience.*

The intent of this book is not to be a laborious reading and memorization resource, but a visual resource for generating technique and process ideas for hand-sketching presentations that may be required of the designer throughout the design process. Computer technology is obviously here to stay and will continually be improved upon and expanded. As designers, we will use technology to our advantage in our fast-paced educational environment and also to meet professional project demands. Nevertheless, the demand for design students education and entry-level designers in the workforce to have the skill of hand-sketching techniques and the understanding of the types of process drawings needed to convey "concept" prior to computer-generated final documents is just as important. Interior design and architecture programs worldwide have supported and continue to support hand-sketching throughout the design process. In fact the NCIDQ (National Council of Interior Design Qualification) still require hand drafting and sketching techniques as the method of exam documentation. Through informal surveying of interior design and architectural practitioners, the author can unequivocally state that the industry professionals embrace and sometimes require entry-level and seasoned designers to obtain an effective skill in hand-sketched "rough" line drawings to the various 2 and 3-dimensional illustrations to convey their concept ideas.

The topics covered in Ideation Chapters 2, 3, and 4 include *bubble diagramming, quick grid scaling for creating 2 and 3-dimensional "ideation" sketches, space plan blocking, schematic plans and elevations, various types of quick perspective drawing techniques, and millwork and furnishing concept sketches* Ideation Chapter 5 addresses sketch enhancements using *delineation techniques, light source considerations, and color.* Ideation Chapter 6 covers the topics of including "written" information and *line graphics* to convey font styling using standard "architectural" and "custom" lettering techniques with further visual enhancements of added *color,* and final thoughts of factors that influence the level of visual enhancements to the sketch in the decision-making process are discussed in Ideation Chapter 7.

In Ideation Chapter 8 the author has compiled a "portfolio" of helpful illustration applications for both residential and commercial projects to view as visual references in the designer's pursuit of technique development and decision-making for appropriate presentation sketches. A list of suggested sketching medium resources is available for the designer in Ideation Chapter 9, while Ideation Chapter 10 has a series of copy-right free line drawings to explore hand-sketching techniques and referenced back to the topics covered throughout each chapter and suggested exercises for practice.

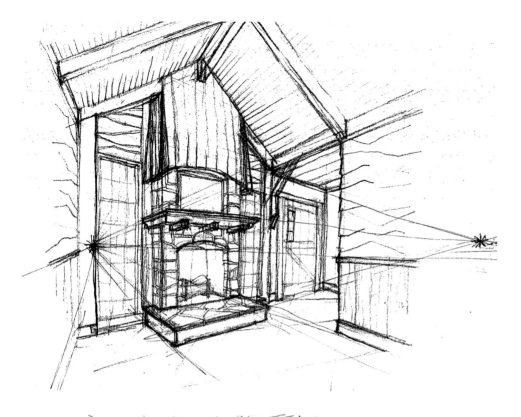

No matter what profession we are inspired to engage in, one must be passionate about the profession; its tasks and benefits, perseverance in learning, and practice the skills endlessly.

Whether the student designer is creating a "line drawing" or "color-rendered illustration," one should strive for <u>visually clear work and precision</u> in technique to convey the best understanding of concepts to the viewer.

Ideation Chapter 2 will discuss various types of sketches that may be required as project drawings transform to "design development" and "portfolio-ready" illustrations through a **Design Continuum Process.**

So, let's begin to explore and embrace the "communication art" of hand-sketching!

Topics covered in Ideation Chapter 2

Overview

Bubble Diagramming

Self-exploration inspiration sketching

Initial concept sketching

Peer review

Design development

Portfolio/marketing

It is important for the student designer to know who their intended reviewer/audience is for presentation of the sketch. This could simply be self-exploration sketching for project inspiration to preparing design development and construction documents that lead to portfolio and marketing illustration opportunities. The graphic below in "Illustration 1" conveys a visual depiction of the **design process** and type of targeted sketch-end product. This chapter will first, address each *continuum step*, and its components with a description and sketch examples to illustrate and help define design process terminology.

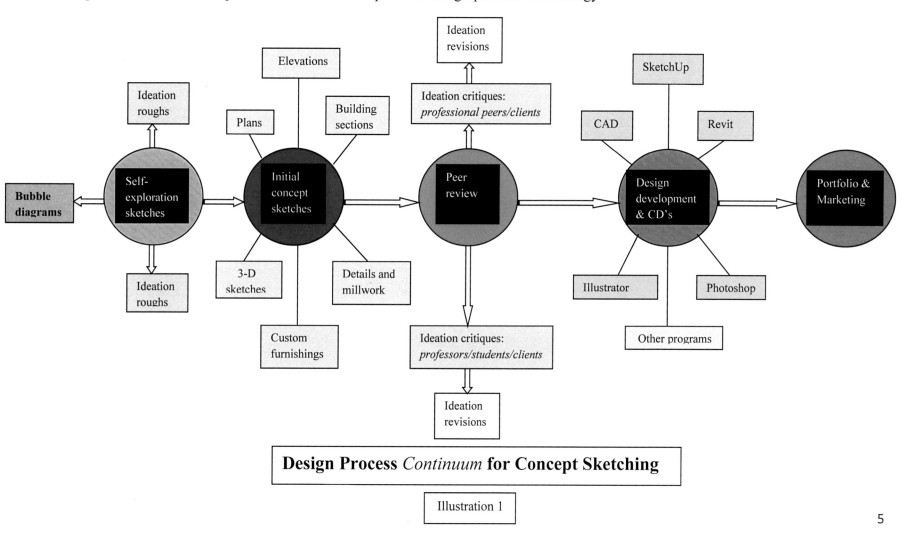

Design Process *Continuum* **for Concept Sketching**

Illustration 1

5

Bubble Diagramming

   The student's educational experience relating to interior design projects typically begins identifying project requirements, usually termed as "the project program." This information is supplied by either the class instructor and/or client sponsor of the student project. The project program is a list of spaces, square footage allotments for those spaces, interior architectural features, material finishes, color suggestions, furnishing requirements, and various building systems to address in the project for a complete end-product- *a successful interior design.*

   This list could also include ideas for creating an image or style for the interior space(s) that will foster a number of *Ideation Roughs* to explore design possibilities. As an example of a "project program" list, we could consider illustrating the first step in graphically portraying the standard components of bubble diagramming symbols that include the following:

> -view considerations
> -space/room allocations (including square feet requirements)
> -space/room adjacency studies
> -circulation/traffic patterns within the spaces
> -special interior features

   Circles and/or elliptical shapes are the industry/educational standard to illustrate graphically bubble diagramming symbolism. And, what we refer to as *"line graphics"* and *"arrows"* to visually connect the various project program component relationships aide in unifying the bubble diagram. *This initial step of bubble diagramming helps establish project precedence and direction in creating <u>ideation sketches</u>* throughout the design process. Bubble diagramming can be applied to any type of design thought process for residential and non-residential projects. So, taking the components of bubble diagramming listed above, one could depict a graphic illustration of the list as indicated on page 7.

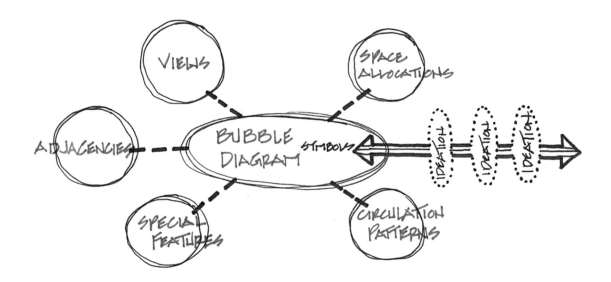

Ideation Chapter 3 will first expand on the graphic components necessary to complete a visual representation of the bubble diagramming process, then, focus on the various illustration techniques of diagramming communication (written information and graphic creativity), including *custom lettering skills*. Again, once the bubble diagramming process has been addressed in a project, the student designer will have a formulation of ideas ready to convey as *ideation roughs* for self-exploration of design possibilities.

To assist one in the many types of sketching techniques, we will look at various 2 and 3-dimensional sketching skills to explore such as grid-scaling, space block plans, and schematic plans and elevations to have a repertoire of sketching alternatives to generate more developed ***initial concept sketches.*** Ideation Chapter 4 will help the student designer develop this skill or be a refresher for some as to the mechanical techniques of 3-dimensional sketching illustrations. Let's continue with a discussion of "self-exploration sketches" and "initial concept sketches" of the Design Process Continuum.

As designers search for inspiration in concept sketching to eventually create their finalized presentation sketch, one may compose a series of *"ideation roughs."* These roughs help to explore the possibilities for the intended design or its constraints. As an example, a cabin retreat living area with a fireplace was a program requirement that had a non-traditional Arts and Crafts style treatment to be considered. "Illustration 2" was an inspirational photo and client drawing that created ideation roughs "Illustration 3 and 4" to develop for a presentation sketch.

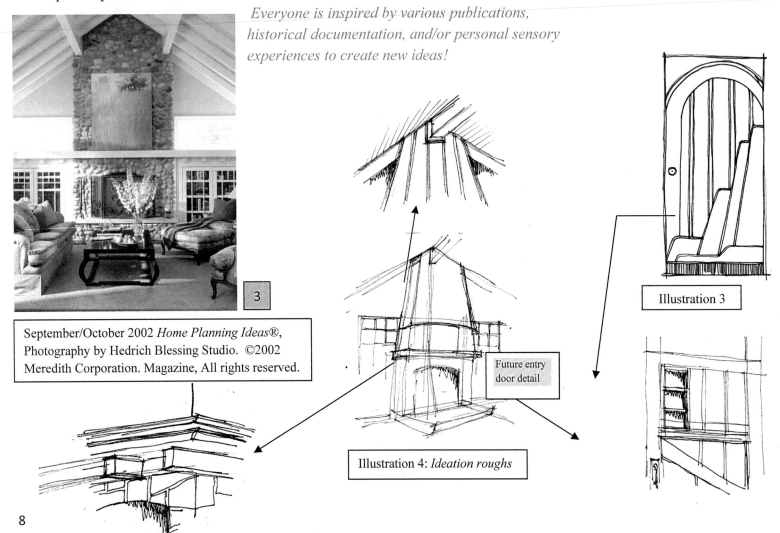

Everyone is inspired by various publications, historical documentation, and/or personal sensory experiences to create new ideas!

3

Illustration 3

Future entry door detail

Illustration 4: *Ideation roughs*

Even during the creation of ideation roughs, designers should be thinking about the detailing of constructed features/components, and their appropriate materials to be used. A free-hand sketching technique is all that is needed in composing rough ideation drawings, no appropriated scale, just a good "eye" for proportions. Ideation Chapter 3 will share the various types of design process sketching techniques that will build on more precise scaling of the illustration(s).

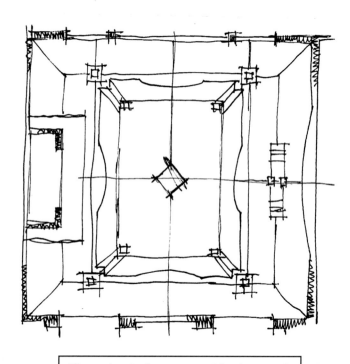

Illustration 5: *floor pattern ideation rough*

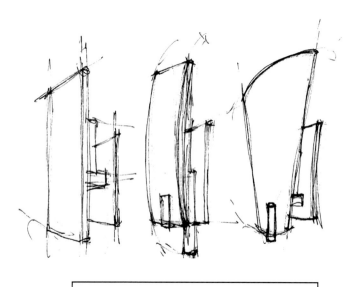

Illustration 6: *light fixture ideation roughs*

The designer may go through multiple ideation roughs for the same feature or component before deciding on which design to develop for the concept illustration.

"Illustrations 7-10" are examples of *ideation roughs* for various projects. Being able to quickly hand-sketch ideas is an acquired skill which will also assist in creating on-site field documents for what the industry terms "as-built" drawings. In turn, these rough sketches of floor plans, elevations, reflected ceiling plans, and featured construction detailing form the basis for design development and final construction documents.

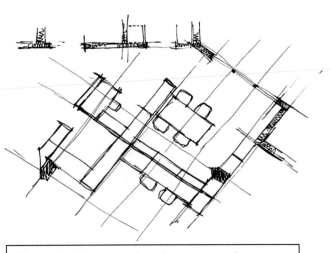

Illustration 7: *systems furnishings space planning*

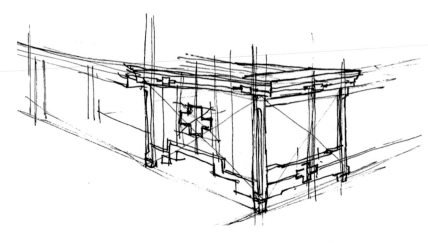

Illustration 8: *custom desk design 3-D*

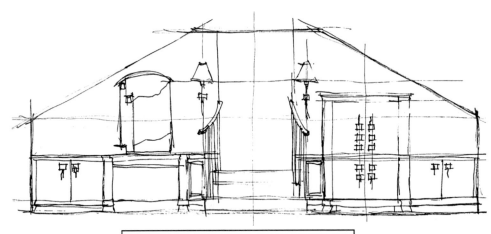

Illustration 9: *master bedroom entry wall*

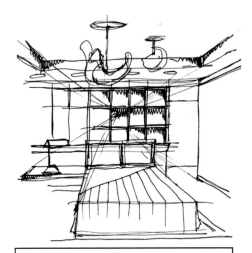

Illustration 10: *hotel suite design 3-D*

Initial concept sketches

After evaluating ideation roughs, one can select the appropriate and most needed one(s) to visually convey the design intent. And these *"initial concept sketches"* lay a strong foundation for design development and options. In design education, it is a good habit to be prepared to sketch options for various components of a project even if the instructor or client does not require them. Options are good discussion motivators and can resolve design issues at the same time, enhancing the design process experience for the designer and project. This shows the viewer the passionate interest of the designer or student designer in making every effort for a successful, enduring, and satisfying project. Interior design education is embracing creating *design options* as enhancing the educational experience and preparing the student designer for the multiple tasks of the professional practice environment in working with the firm's project management and comprehensive design process. So, keeping "optioning!"

> **Suggestion for options:** Compose an original line drawing and overlay the original with trace paper in creating the option sketches. This saves time and energy as shown in "Illustration 11."

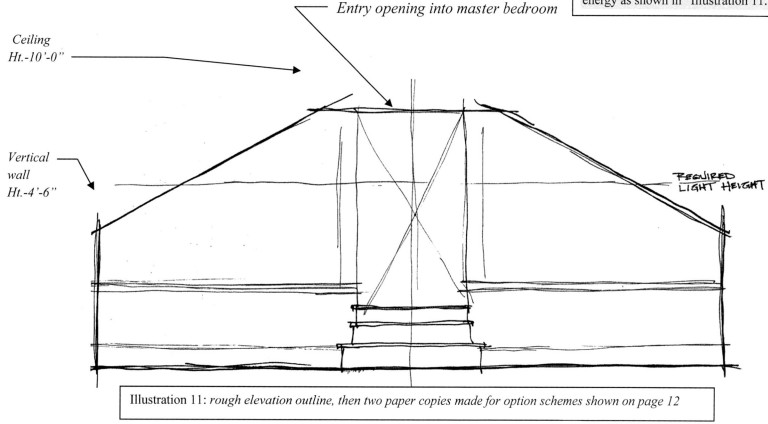

Entry opening into master bedroom

Ceiling Ht.-10'-0"

Vertical wall Ht.-4'-6"

REQUIRED LIGHT HEIGHT

Illustration 11: *rough elevation outline, then two paper copies made for option schemes shown on page 12*

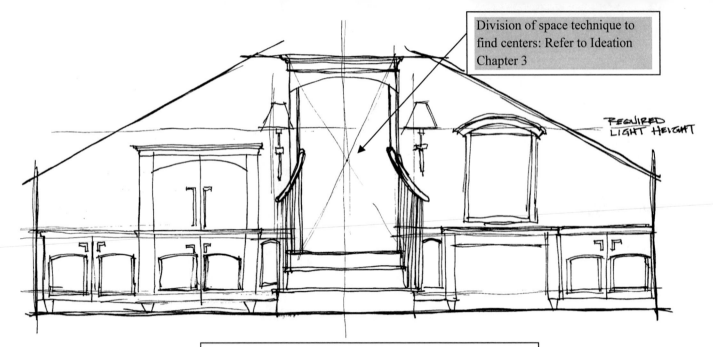

REQUIRED LIGHT HEIGHT

Illustration 12: *elevation option #1 rough- "traditional style"*

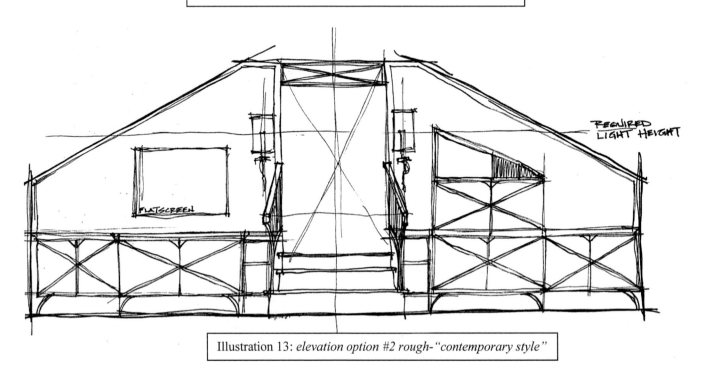

REQUIRED LIGHT HEIGHT

FLATSCREEN

Illustration 13: *elevation option #2 rough-"contemporary style"*

Isometric drawings as illustrated below are easy to compose and show equal detailing emphasis on all surface planes of furniture sketches. This technique of sketching will be addressed in Ideation Chapter 4 and is a widely accepted technique to use with furniture and millwork concepts. It is also a unique way to convey how features and components can be assembled or disassembled.

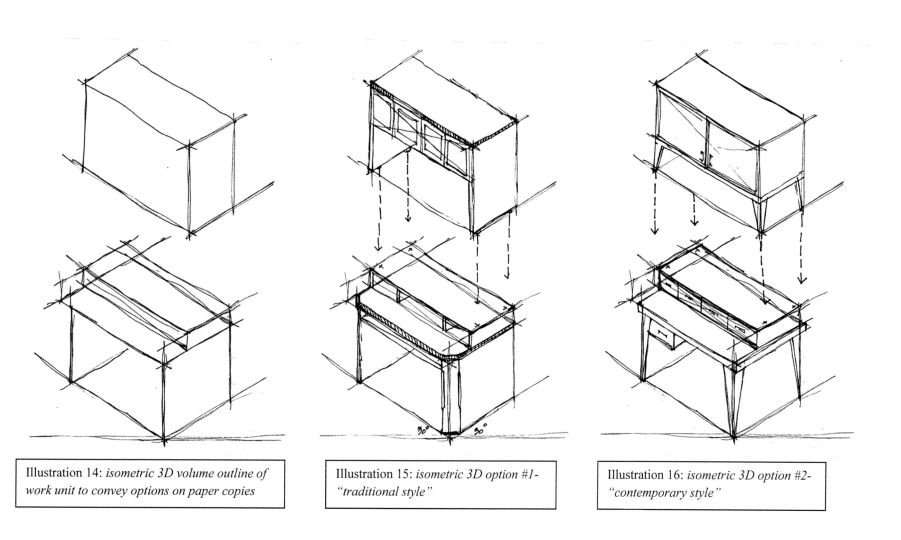

Illustration 14: *isometric 3D volume outline of work unit to convey options on paper copies*

Illustration 15: *isometric 3D option #1- "traditional style"*

Illustration 16: *isometric 3D option #2- "contemporary style"*

When the student designer or professional is ready for peer reviewing of concept sketches, the sketch is taken a little further in regards to visual enhancements and sometimes using **crisper and more refined** feature line work as indicated in the sketched examples below. And, sometimes it may be necessary to delineate (adding material finish simulations) to various surfaces depending on the level of visual understanding of the reviewer. The visual depth and enhancement complexity is covered in Ideation Chapter 7: *"When is Enough, Enough?"* The topic and techniques for visual delineation enhancements are addressed in Ideation Chapter 5.

The following illustrations are suggested examples as visual enhancements for the critiquing process that will assist the designer with any needed revisions to be made prior to final approval of the sketches to develop into a project set of design development and construction documents. Notes are not indicted, but obviously would be necessary to further convey the design concepts to focus on the visual delineation enhancement versions.

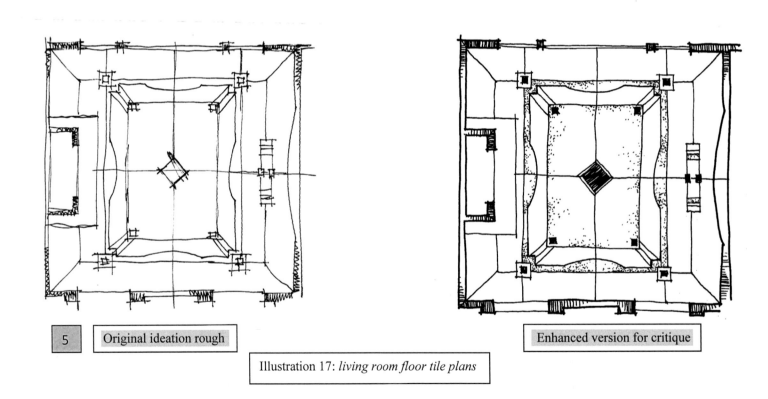

| 5 | Original ideation rough |

Enhanced version for critique

Illustration 17: *living room floor tile plans*

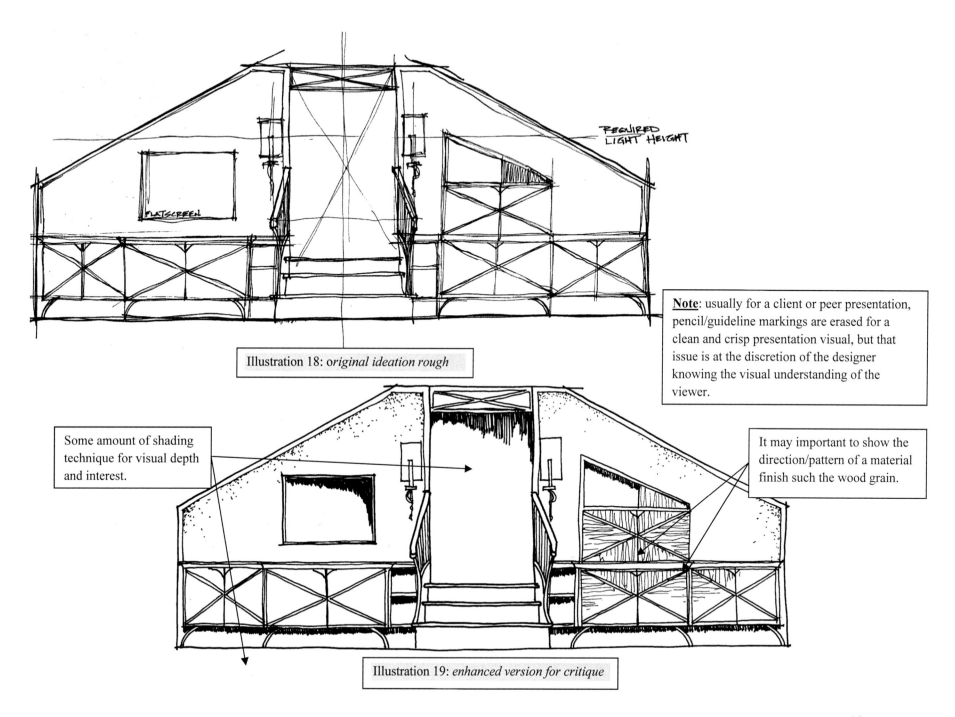

REQUIRED
LIGHT HEIGHT

FLATSCREEN

Illustration 18: *original ideation rough*

Note: usually for a client or peer presentation, pencil/guideline markings are erased for a clean and crisp presentation visual, but that issue is at the discretion of the designer knowing the visual understanding of the viewer.

Some amount of shading technique for visual depth and interest.

It may important to show the direction/pattern of a material finish such the wood grain.

Illustration 19: *enhanced version for critique*

Illustrating furniture, furnishings, and millwork, in some instances,
especially the fact that the sketch is larger than other types of drawings,
the visual surface detailing could be more developed in order to convey the
concept as in "Illustration 20 and 21" below.

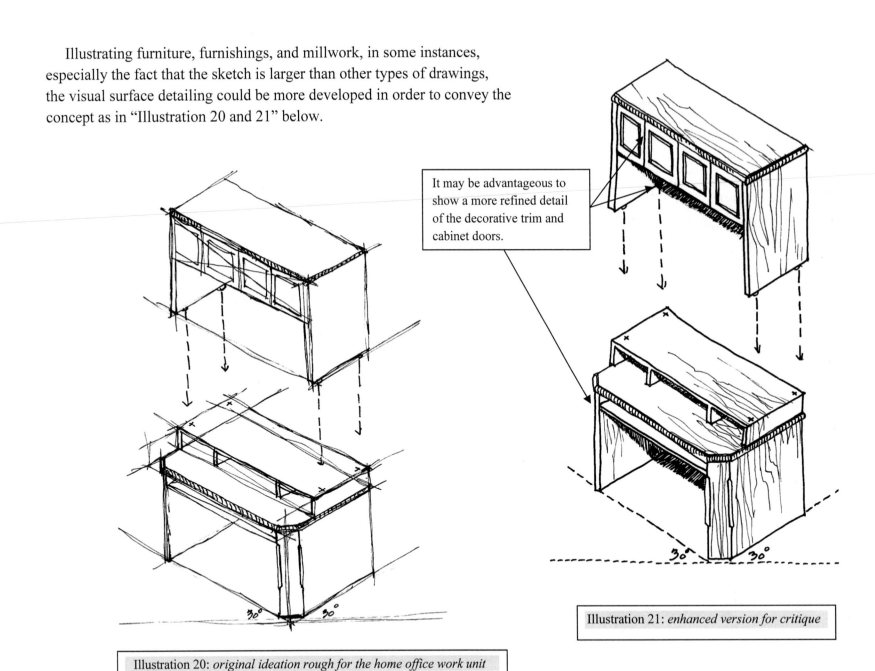

It may be advantageous to
show a more refined detail
of the decorative trim and
cabinet doors.

Illustration 21: *enhanced version for critique*

Illustration 20: *original ideation rough for the home office work unit*

Design development and construction documents (CD's)

The ideation critiquing process can be time consuming and tedious, but is a necessary process to achieve the desired goals for the project and/or client. Once revisions are made to all types of concept sketches/preliminary drawings, and the approvals have been granted to the designer, whatever level of one's career status, then typically, the final design development drawings are incorporated into a set(s) of construction documents (CD's). This process is done through various means, including computer-aided (CAD) resources, such as AutoCAD, Revit, Sketch-up, Illustrator, and Photoshop, to mention some of these standard office documentation practices. But, what has been discussed in Ideation Chapters 1 and 2, idea roughs, concept sketches, and process critiques and revisions through hand-sketching skills will enhance the concept thought processes.

There is a wealth of resources to share with the student designer and practitioner such as computer-aided documentation techniques, typical drawings to include in a CD set/package, and the visual composition of these documents, but is beyond the scope of this publication resource. The topic of computer-aided drawings was needed to be mentioned because it being an important tool in the preparation of professional documents and its use in the design development process. The author uses both hand-sketching and CAD-generated drawings, both in the classroom and professional practice.

Portfolio and marketing

It is important to note that some developed hand sketched presentation drawings are worthy of student portfolio examples, because they will show to the potential employer ones skill in creating and understanding the *design process.* Company/firm interviewers do like to see these types of drawings in portfolio presentations as well as the "finished" technical documents for projects, finish sample boards, and additional complementary work examples. So, keep some of the best hand-sketched process drawings, and enhance them even more if you want to showcase this skill; use the skill as a marketing tool for you. This is also appropriate and an opportunity for the practicing professional to highlight their expertise in **design process** and **concept development** through their various means of marketing media. The next and last page of this chapter share a collage of portfolio and marketing quality hand-sketched illustrations of the author and former students (noted); and all drawings started from *"ideation roughs."* Ideation Chapter 8 includes an expanded *"Portfolio of illustration applications for both residential and commercial projects."*

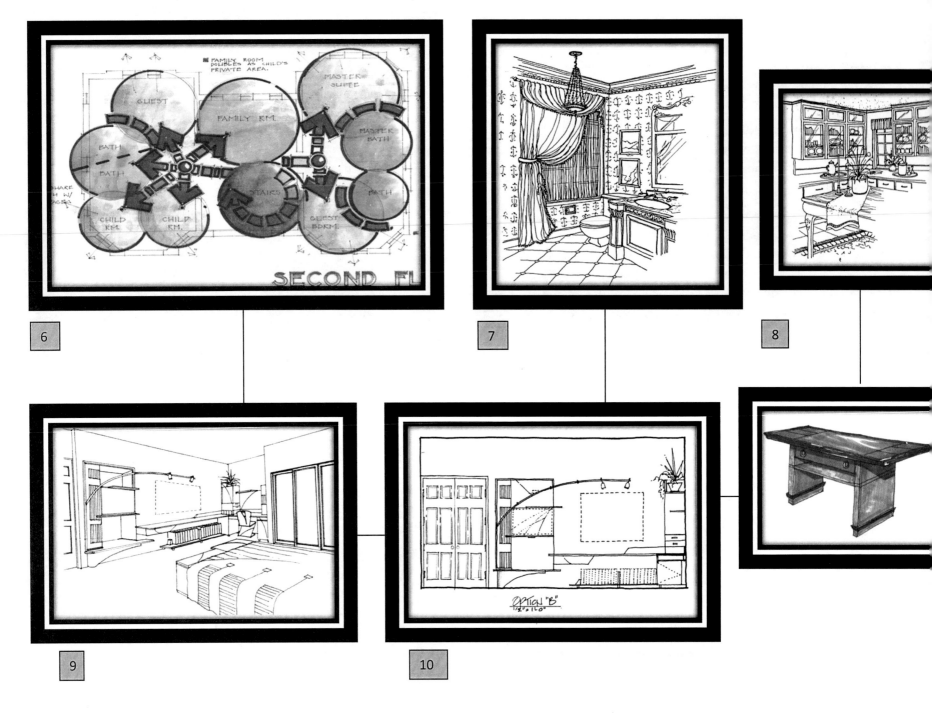

6

7

8

9

10

18

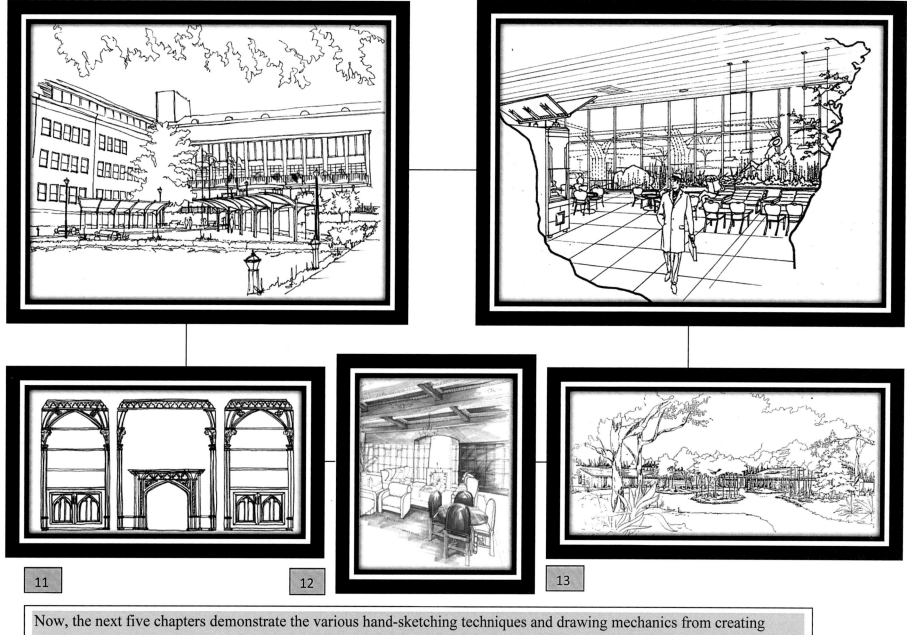

Now, the next five chapters demonstrate the various hand-sketching techniques and drawing mechanics from creating rough sketches to portfolio-ready and quality presentation illustrations. So, let's be passionate, practice, persevere, and have fun!

Topics covered in Ideation Chapter 3

Bubble Diagrams

Diagramming symbol shapes and sizing

Written information

Graphic creativity

Custom lettering techniques

Color and enhancement applications

Grid scaling

Space block plans

Schematic plans and elevations

Ideation Chapter 3

Bubble diagrams

Bubble diagram illustrations are fundamental to the design process, no matter what phase or type of project undertaken. There are various opinions within the educational communities regarding the diagramming symbol sizes and shapes, the type and amount of visual information depicted, graphic creativity, and color. This chapter will identify and explain these issues in order for one to develop their own system and level of skill in bubble diagramming illustrating.

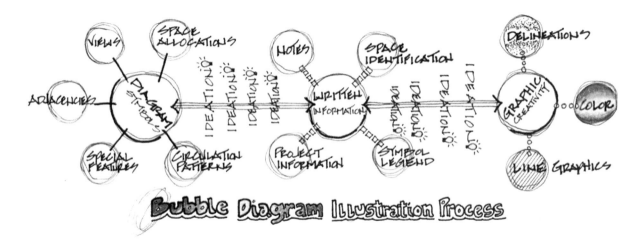

Any type of illustration, including bubble diagrams, from "rough conceptual thinking" to "portfolio presentation quality" should address visual and written information clarity and readability. Going through the bubble diagramming process will generate _ideation_ inspiration for the project concept and design development, and creating several bubble diagram options will help define and determine the best solution(s) for the project. Because, the first concept may not always be the best solution – expand your thinking with diagramming options. Illustration 1, above, is a graphic depiction of the expanded components of bubble diagramming illustration using **the bubble diagram** technique. Now, let's move onto the mechanics, visual graphics, and written information associated with creating bubble diagrams.

Diagramming symbol shapes and sizing

The educational and professional practice diagramming shape has been the "circle." Each circle is a representation of a space or area within the design project and should be proportional to the intended size of the space based on square footage allocations. When beginning an illustration, one can use an architectural scale/circle template to determine a bubble shape size as a guide for the rest of the space allocation bubbles. Do not let this simple initial step be a drawing "crutch" because you may not have a building shell floor plan as a visual reference if the project itself is highly conceptual or a particular floor plan/building space has not been determined. The student, building on their bubble diagramming skills, should begin to envision proportional bubble sizing strategies for square footage allotments based on a design project program.

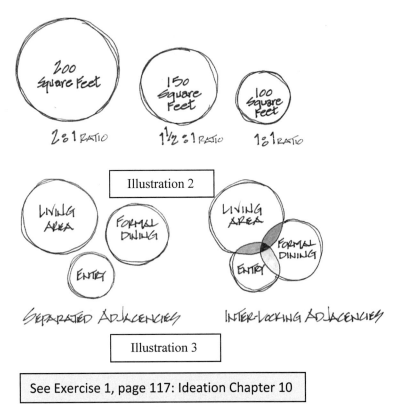

Space allocations
Start with any size free-hand circle and enlarge/reduce in proportioned ratios the circles to represent square foot allocations of space requirements.

Adjacencies
Space allocations then need to be located graphically using the determined program requirements for "functional proximities." These spatial groupings can be illustrated as separate adjacencies or interlocking adjacencies. (Note: an advantage of the interlocking adjacencies can show visually the level of proportional importance of the adjacency.)

See Exercise 1, page 117: Ideation Chapter 10

Circulation patterns

Two types of graphic illustrations for circulation/traffic patterns within a bubble diagram that have consistently been used are *primary and secondary* relationships. Primary illustrations can also be considered "public access" and secondary illustrations can be considered "private access" for either residential or non-residential projects. These graphic symbols are used as *directional connectors* between space allocation bubbles. Examples in Illustration 4 can be used as primary or secondary circulation as long as each is identified in a symbol legend key discussed in **"Written Information"**. Students are encouraged to develop their own types of graphic symbols keeping in mind to be consistent in use of the symbols and not to overpower the bubble diagram with artistic quality.

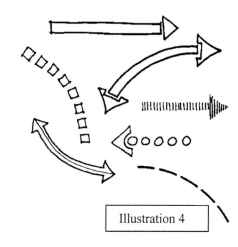

Illustration 4

See Exercise 2, page 118: Ideation Chapter 10

View indications

The project program may emphasize the importance of a particular view or views in relation to the space allocation bubbles. This can be done by simply placing a similar graphic representation as depicted in Illustration 5 just outside of the diagram bubble for that particular space allocation. Again, students can graphically experiment with types of illustrations to use but not to overpower the presentation.

Special features

Design focal points such as a fireplace, stairs, level changes, media center, skylights, etc. should just be noted for a bubble diagram. A representative shape and proportional size for such components would be more appropriately depicted on a space block plan or schematic floor plan diagram.

Illustration 5

See Exercise 3, page 119: Ideation Chapter 10

Written information

Space identification

Free-hand lettering for each space allocation bubble must be identified as indicated in Illustration 3. Just be consistent in space title names so not to confuse the viewer and an appropriate lettering size proportional to the bubble size. Sometimes it may be necessary to letter beyond the bubble shape, which is acceptable, but again be consistent visually.

Notes

If there are some significant features or information necessary to communicate to the viewer at this conceptual stage of the design illustration process, *be selective*. (Save some of your information for the oral presentation). The scale of note information, as a general rule, should be approximately one-third (1/3) the height of space titles.

Symbol legend

Creating a symbol legend for the bubble diagram is just as important as all design development and construction drawing documents. The symbol legend should include *circulation/traffic patterns,* indicating **primary and secondary** relationships, and again, could be identifying public and private relationships, intended important *view* identification, and any other visually needed graphic symbol. The words "circulation and/or traffic patterns" could be added to the legend description. Graphic arrows (as shown in Illustration 4) added to either or both ends of the circulation pattern symbols can help define the importance of direction flow of the circulation and room space allocation.

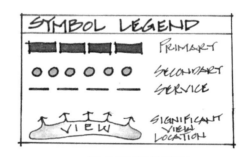

Illustration 6

Project/client information

Identify the project and/or client name, project location (if known), date, and reference to a drawing number, such as *"Concept Bubble Diagram #1,"* for record keeping purposes. As shown on "Illustration 7" to the right, hand-lettered information could be standard architecturally-trained styling (7a) or custom lettering, or a combination of both (7b). Custom hand-lettering is further discussed in "Graphic Creativity" below.

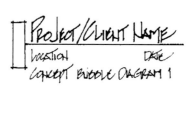

Illustration 7a

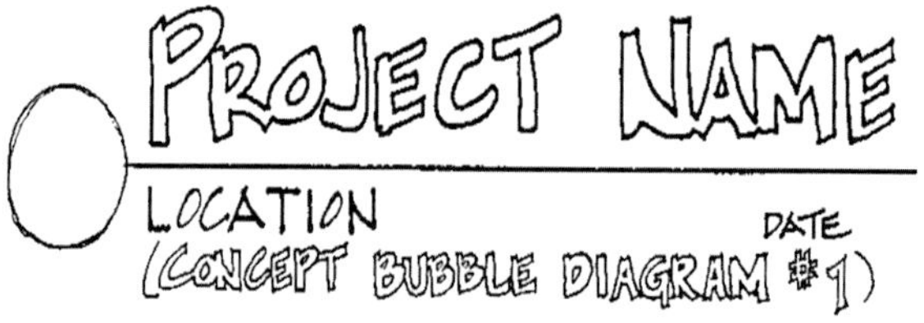

Illustration 7b

Graphic Creativity

Line graphics

Using *"line graphics"* as well as *"delineations"* discussed in the following section is a choice of the student designer. The author uses both to emphasize certain diagramming components that are deemed important based on the project program and written information being conveyed depicted in <u>Illustration 8a (underscoring space names)</u> <u>and 8b (accenting titles)</u> respectively. *Varying graphic "line weights" can help in emphasizing illustration information also.*

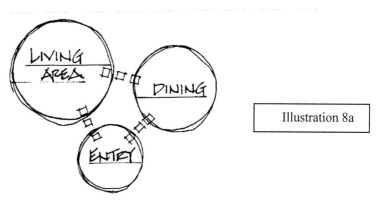

Illustration 8a

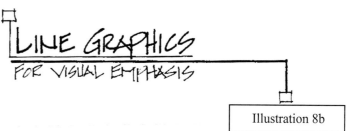

Illustration 8b

25

Delineations

 Students may be familiar with various delineation
techniques for visual enhancements in any type
of illustration; the most common ones are depicted in
Illustration 9a, 9b, and 9c. Dots or "pointillism," lines,
cross-hatching, and combination of the three can be
used to accent/emphasize diagram bubbles, project
title information (Illustrations 9a and 9b respectively).

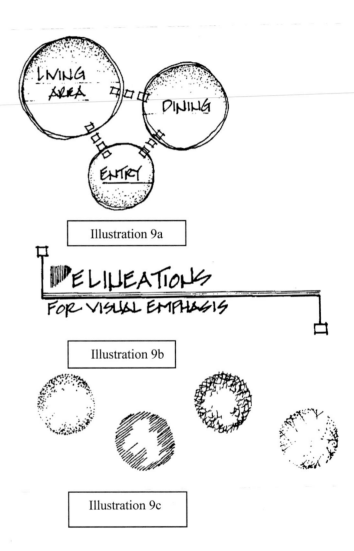

Illustration 9a

Illustration 9b

Illustration 9c shows an example of the common
delineations used for any graphic representation.
Again, the student should experiment and practice
delineations; you may create your own style(s).

Illustration 9c

See Exercise 4, page 120: Ideation Chapter 10

26

Custom lettering techniques

Students can create their unique lettering style, specifically for project title information, sub-titles, and student name/class/school information using an "under-lay guide" that is hand-lettered on another sheet of paper (author prefers "bond/copy" paper). Using light guide lines also for all lettered information is essential for height and style consistency, and proportional correctness. Create the lettering guide styles using a medium to wide-tip felt marker or pen for a variety of size and visual style from all upper case to upper/lower case letters, and from architecturally-trained lettering to more "boxed" type lettering as depicted in Illustration 10. Experiment!

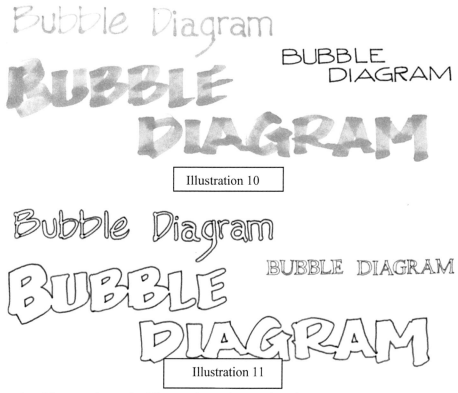

Illustration 10

Illustration 11

Then, using lettered guides as above in Illustration 10, overlay tissue paper or sometimes bond copy paper will suffice as long you can see the letter images beneath, and line trace the letters to create the desired graphic look as depicted in Illustration 11. Check out various copy-right free font styles to trace over for additional letter graphic uniqueness.

See Exercise 5, page 121: Ideation Chapter 10

Color and enhancement applications

The use of color in any illustration application always draws the attention of the viewer, focusing in on a particular feature or group of features. Color in bubble diagramming should always be used to help visually organize the composition, identify functional groupings and associations, highlight a significant project program component, and/or visually stimulate written graphic information. In addition to color being a visual stimulant, it can also inspire or be inspiring through "ideation" processes envisioning potential color schemes for the project setting the stage for further design development and presentation discussions. But, grayed neutral schemes with various delineations have been quite successful visually, that has a "professional finished" appeal to them. Illustration 12 below is an example of color enhancement possibilities for both diagramming bubbles and written information. The next page shows two bubble diagram scenarios incorporating illustration process sketching techniques discussed in this chapter.

See Exercise 6, page 122: Ideation Chapter 10

Illustration 12

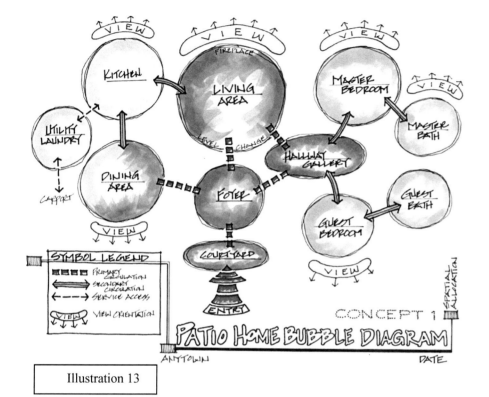

Illustration 13

Illustration 13: *A neutral color scheme would be appropriate in identifying the spatial allocations only when "color" is not an influential factor at this stage of the design process,* as in this residential project scenario example created by a list of predetermined client program requirements.

-using three color hues of cool grays and re-emphasizing each bubble perimeter with the same cool gray marker.

-the dining area, in both illustrations, has two different color applications to convey both "service" and "social/community/public" spaces

-remember to use very light guide lines for all lettered information (4H or non-photo blue pencil leads), and erase them before adding color

Illustration 14: *Color in bubble diagramming is important when "color" is an influential visual and project program factor (i.e., complement the presentation color scheme or assist in emphasizing spatial allocation groupings)*

-additional shading delineations in each bubble (i.e., light lavender pencil over the yellow-gold and aqua green bubbles help to not only distinguish those groupings but also reinforces the "secondary/service/private" circulation relationships)

-living area, foyer, and dining area have "pointillism" delineation to emphasize those functional areas

-hallway/gallery has angular linear line delineation to emphasize a unique project program requirement

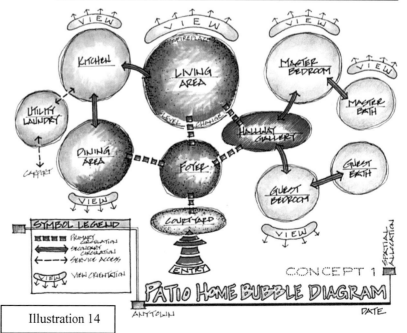

Illustration 14

29

Grid Scaling for 2 and 3-dimensional illustrations

<u>2-dimensional grids:</u>

The term "grid scaling" is a technique to create a guide in developing two and three-dimensional hand sketches without mechanical drawing skills that can take valuable time during the design process. One must have the basic knowledge of these mechanical drawing skills to understand and develop the free-hand sketching techniques. The professional design community and practicum still do embrace and sometimes require these skills from the student intern and/or the design graduate entering their professional career in order to create quick sketches for their firm's project meetings and to assist the client in the design process prior to design development and construction documents. When multiple concepts are needed to be addressed, hand-sketched illustrations can save time and budget dollars. Illustrations 15, 16, 17 below are examples of proportional "grid scaling" to use for 2-dimensional plans, elevations, sections, and details. The next page will show sketching applications.

Illustration 16

Dotted lines in original block to find center point, then dashed lines, horizontally and vertically to divide block. Then a line from point 1 through mid-point 2 intersecting extended top block line to find 3 which is the next equal block module width. Continue the horizontal and vertical lines to create as many grid blocks as needed.

Lines 1-4 were sketched first for horizontal proportions and lines A-D vertically to finish the module widths. Each square can represent any size module (1, 2, 5 feet square) as an example.

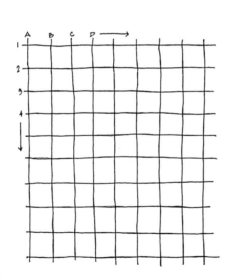

Illustration 15

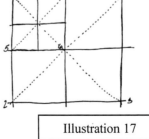

Illustration 17

<u>Dividing a large block</u> (points 1-4) into equal areas:

Dotted lines corner-to-corner with a horizontal and vertical line through the intersecting dashed lines divide the square into four equal modules. Then repeat the process as in block 1,5,6,7 to create smaller grid scaling as needed.

2-dimensional grid scaling applications

   (Remember to use a 4H or non-photo blue pencil leads for all grid guidelines and lettered information-*this creates consistency and overall neatness for your work*)
Both sketches in Illustration 18 & 19 use the same grid setup as in Illustration 15 on the previous page. The office plan sketch in Illustration 18 uses the grid as 2-foot square modules and base and upper cabinet elevation in Illustration 19 the grid represents 1-foot square modules. The noted dimensions show using the different grid scaling modules how one can proportionally "guesstimate" various dimensions.

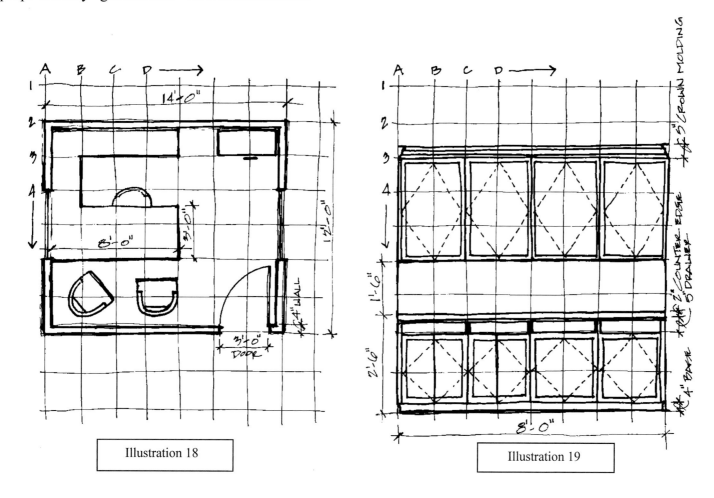

| Illustration 18 | Illustration 19 |

3-dimensional grids:

Using and understanding one and two-point perspective mechanical drafting techniques, one can easily set up quick 3-dimensional grid guides to use for sketching. And, again, no architectural scale is required in setting up these types of grid scaling guides. A review of a one-point perspective is shown below in Illustration 20 and quick sketch application in Illustration 21.

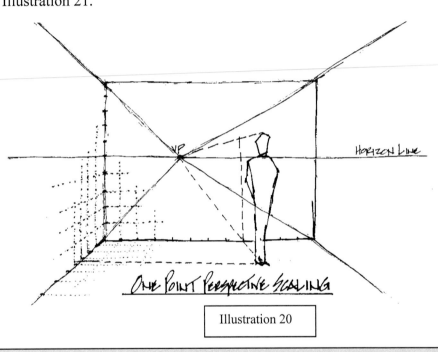

ONE POINT PERSPECTIVE SCALING

Illustration 20

Illustration 20

The back wall is drawn first in a one-point perspective and the grid modules are created on the space surface by one of the methods in Illustrations 16 and 17, or simply "eyeballing" the proportional grids. *(size of the wall turned out to be 12 feet wide by 10 feet high)*

-Then deciding on the horizon line and vanishing point (VP), one can create the grid modules on all surfaces of the interior space indicated by the dotted lines.

- And, extending lines through all four wall corners create floor and ceiling lines.

-The person is located 8 feet from the left and 3.5 feet out from the back wall.

Illustration 21

Sketchy line work is shown below the horizon line to locate features proportionally correct. *Remember that one sees the tops of surfaces below the horizon line and the underside of surfaces above the horizon line.*

-Always check your lines of perspective correctness with the vanishing point located.

-The darkened (varied felt tip lines) above the horizon line show the potential for a more finished look to the sketch that will be discussed in detail in Ideation Chapter 4 and Chapter 5 "Delineation Enhancements".

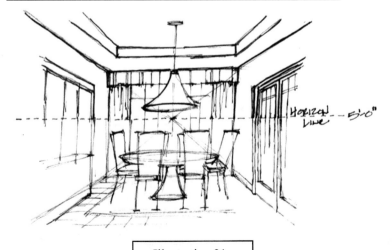

Illustration 21

A review of two-point perspective is shown below in Illustration 22. A detailed discussion and finished drawing examples will be shown in Ideation Chapter 5 "Delineation Enhancements" and Ideation Chapter 8 "Portfolio of Illustration Applications."

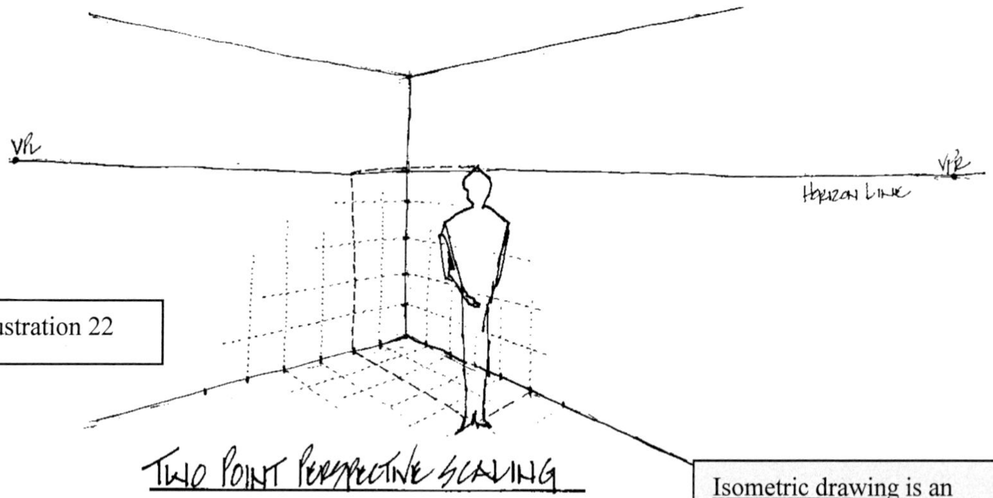

Two-point perspectives always start will drawing a line to represent any "true corner" of the space, determining the number of grid divisions on that line to represent "feet" dimensioning.

-Then, using one of the methods for creating grid modules on the space surfaces similar to a one-point perspective and location of the horizon line, vanishing points left (VPL) and right (VPR), and "eye-balling" foot increments from the "true corner" to finish grid scaling, the drawing guide is ready for drawing exploration.

-Remember to experiment locating the vanishing points (not too close to the "true corner") so the drawing looks proportionally correct.

Illustration 22

TWO POINT PERSPECTIVE SCALING

Isometric drawing is an excellent technique to illustrate furniture pieces and enlarged interior and architectural detailing components.

-The initial 3-D "box" is drawn at a 30-degree orientation off a horizontal guideline and scaling divisions are created using one of the methods previously discussed as shown in Illustration 23.

-Illustration 24 shows an application for a "Tansu" unit.

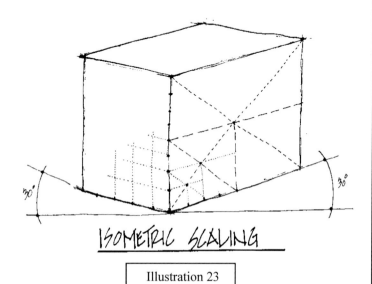

ISOMETRIC SCALING

Illustration 23

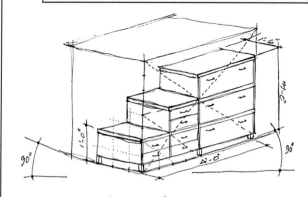

TANSU STORAGE UNIT
UTILIZING ISOMETRIC GRID SCALING

Illustration 24

33

Space Block Plans

The experience gained in bubble diagramming and grid scaling is essential when further developing project concepts in relationship to space planning. The "space block plan(s)" is similar to the *schematic layout* phase prior to creating a preliminary floor plan. This type of process drawing is a standard planning aide in commercial projects, but is useful in large-scale residential projects as well. It is an illustration that defines space allotments within a supplied floor plan for the design project, usually with color applications designating the required program functional areas, and various notes and labeling system. The look of a hand sketched space block plan still conveys conceptual thinking and development. CAD (computer aided drafting) programs can achieve the same process, but a more "finished" appeal to the presentation. Illustration 25 is an example floor plan shell that may be furnished for a project, and Illustration 26a depicts the first step of a space block plan solution identifying square footage allotments for intended spaces prior to illustrating "sub-sets" of individual space requirements as show in Illustration 26a on the following page 35.

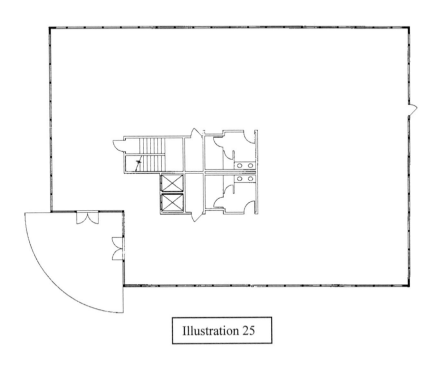

Illustration 25

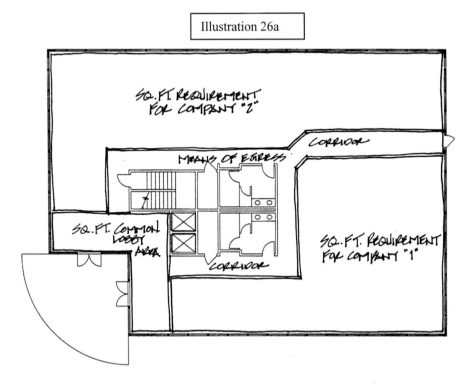

Illustration 26a

Illustration 26b below conveys a finished space block plan with all "sub-sets" of individual project space requirements "to scale" in relation to the building shell floor plan. In this example, the monochromatic color scheme with varied light and dark hues designates the individual "company" office areas. The use of color and line delineation helps to differentiate between office areas, *means of egress (corridors),* and common lobby area. And, for visual clarity and impact, the center core of elevators, restrooms, stairs, and storage compartments are left uncolored.

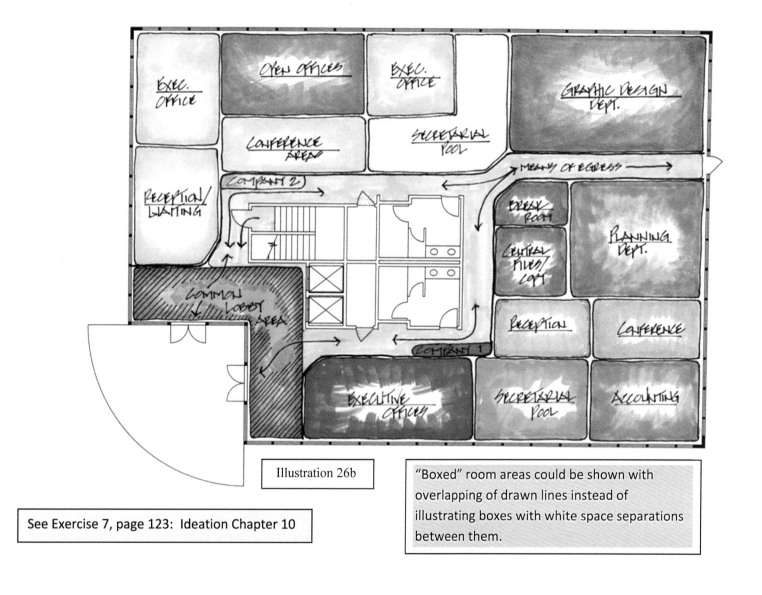

Illustration 26b

"Boxed" room areas could be shown with overlapping of drawn lines instead of illustrating boxes with white space separations between them.

See Exercise 7, page 123: Ideation Chapter 10

35

Schematic plans and elevations

Hand-sketched presentation floor plan techniques can also be utilized in documenting what the design profession calls "as-built" drawings. All designers, interior and architectural students and professionals, are required to have knowledge and skills in documenting an existing space if a set of plans are not available to use for a project. So, whether a student or professional project, one may need to visit a building site and create an as-built drawing(s) that identifies wall and interior partition locations, doors and door swings, windows/glazing, power and communication outlets, plumbing fixtures, built-in millwork, heating, ventilating, and air conditioning sources, ceiling detailing, and sometimes significant elevation feature illustrations. And, usually, dimensions need to be identified with the as-built information. The hand-sketched creation of concept, presentation, and/or as-built plans and elevations is an important skill to acquire to assist in design process illustrations in order to compile information for final CAD generated documents. Whichever type of sketched drawing is required, and the drawing needs to have *"scaled correctness";* the use of grid scaling would be appropriate. The following illustration steps use grid scaling in creating the various floor plan steps for a final hand-sketched presentation drawing.

STEP 1	STEP 2

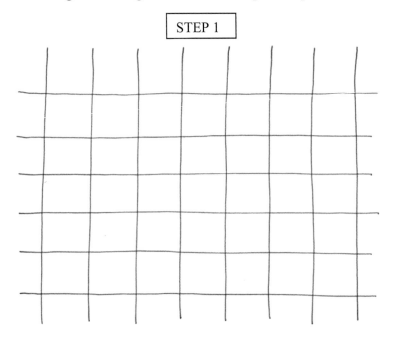

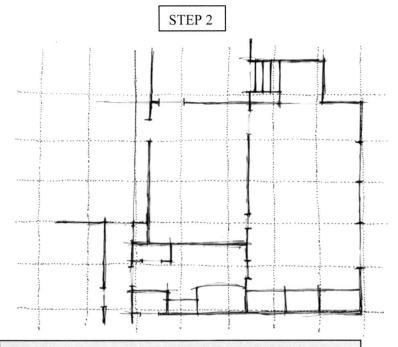

Illustration 27 shows the basic grid scaling guide that represents 4'-0" modules for a home renovation project.

Illustration 28 shows using the grid line scaling guide (dotted lines) for the initial location of interior partitions/doors/windows. *Always use multiple "sketchy" line work to locate all features.*

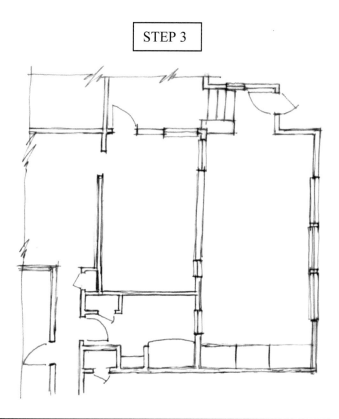

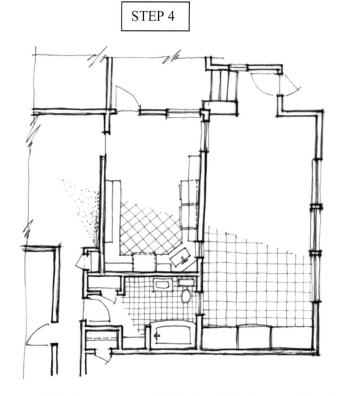

Illustration 29 above shows the definition of all the correct locations and "to scale" interior partitions/doors/windows/ built-in millwork using a bolder (thicker) felt-tip over the sketchy line work. Constantly check yourself with the grid guidelines to verify dimensional correctness.

If documenting an "as-built" drawing; locations of power and communication outlets, light fixtures/switching, and heating, ventilating, and air conditioning sources can be shown for future construction documents.

Illustration 30 above shows a limited reference to various types of floor coverings. Surface delineation types and illustrations will be covered in Ideation Chapter 5.

Remember to vary the felt-tip and/or pencil line weights using a hierarchy of feature importance. As a suggestion: *major feature lines and titles should be the heaviest line weight, built-in millwork/door swings/windows and notes should be medium line weight, and surface delineations the lightest line weight.*

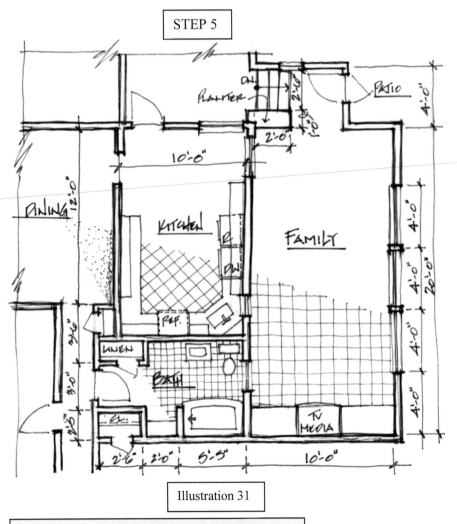

STEP 5

Illustration 31

See Exercise 8, page 124: Ideation Chapter 10

Illustration 31 shows a finalized version of the floor plan renovation with major dimensions, room titles, and various feature identifications. One could choose to delineate, (sometimes called "pochette") the walls and interior partitions for added visual impact and spatial definition. These delineation types will be discussed and illustrated in Ideation Chapter 5.

Suggestion: *Try not to overpower the sketch with floor material delineations, just indicate a proportion of the intended or existing floor surfaces. One may choose to delineate more area if depicting a detailed floor covering presentation plan that has various design line work needed to be conveyed. Your design judgment and/or project requirement stipulations would be the determining factor(s) regarding the issue of how much to visually portray.*

Illustration 32 on the following page is an example of a larger project hand-sketched plan for a conceptual presentation including furniture arrangements.

In creating scaling correctness, it is always advisable to either create your own grid guide if one is not supplied to you, especially at "on-site" documentation visits, or use a supplied/purchased grid. Then, just determine what each grid module dimension needs to be represented and start sketching the document using trace paper and/or a sketch pad.

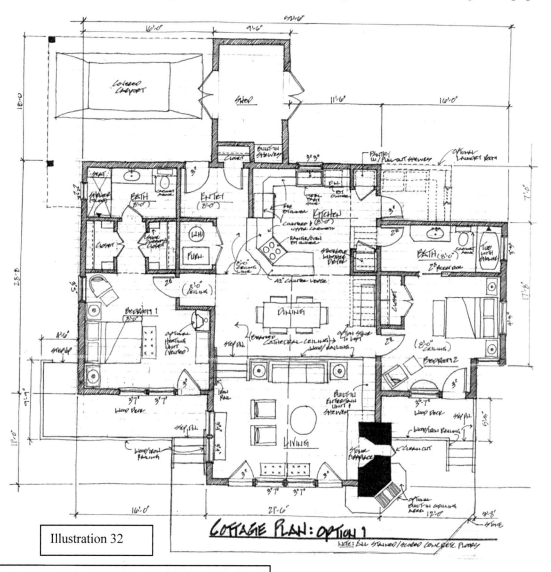

Illustration 32

The grid module guidelines can still faintly be seen (each grid module unit represented 1'-0" square feet) and most of the "sketchy" line work has been covered with various black felt-tip line weights according to the previously mentioned line hierarchy.

The exterior walls and interior partitions have been delineated graphically using 45 degree lines.

There is no floor covering delineations, because as noted, the floor material is stained concrete. (Scoring pattern will be determined)

One can erase some or the majority of the pencil guidelines as illustrated with this example. This is at the discretion of the designer if one feels that the multiple sketchy line work would be distracting for a final conceptual presentation.

Suggestion: *The use of black felt-tip is a good illustration tool for visual impact and clarity especially when copies are needed or sending via email.*

See Exercise 9, page 125: Ideation Chapter 10

Sketching an elevation, similar steps are followed as in plan illustrations, but usually the grid guideline modules represented are smaller because of the potential feature detailing that can be conveyed. A *1-foot square grid* would be appropriate for such detail scaling as Illustration 33 shows for Step 1. In Step 2, Illustration 34, block out the main features first, locating the feature component dimensional correctness.

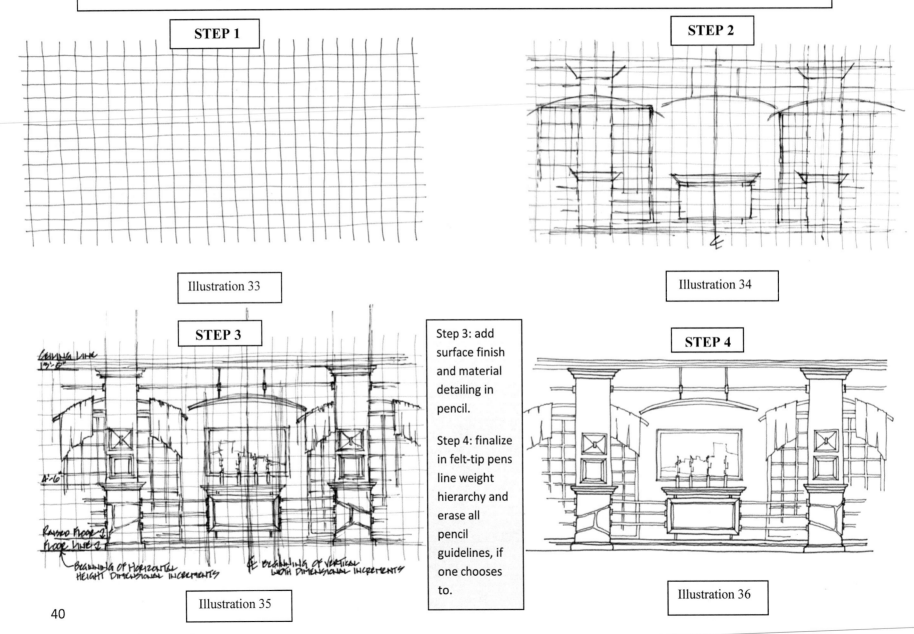

STEP 1

Illustration 33

STEP 2

Illustration 34

STEP 3

Illustration 35

Step 3: add surface finish and material detailing in pencil.

Step 4: finalize in felt-tip pens line weight hierarchy and erase all pencil guidelines, if one chooses to.

STEP 4

Illustration 36

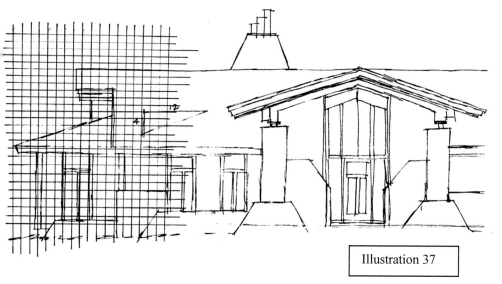

In the exterior home elevation to the left, Illustration 37, the partial grid (for visual clarity of instruction) is represented as *1-foot squares* also for architectural detailing. Block in the major features for correct dimensional proportions prior to illustrating surface material building products in detail.

Illustration 37

Illustration 38 starts to depict surface material delineation detailing such as wood components, stone, and some planting delineations.

Illustration 39 shows a final rendition drawing with erased guidelines and the use of heavier line weights for foreground features.

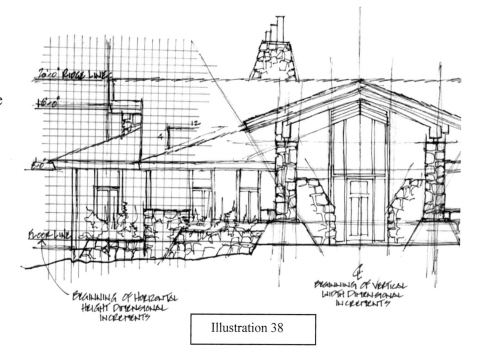

Illustration 38

It is important to note in creating **_visual depth_** to any illustration, heavy line weights will emphasize features and components that are closer to the viewer. Surface material delineation detailing will be enhanced in Ideation Chapter 5.

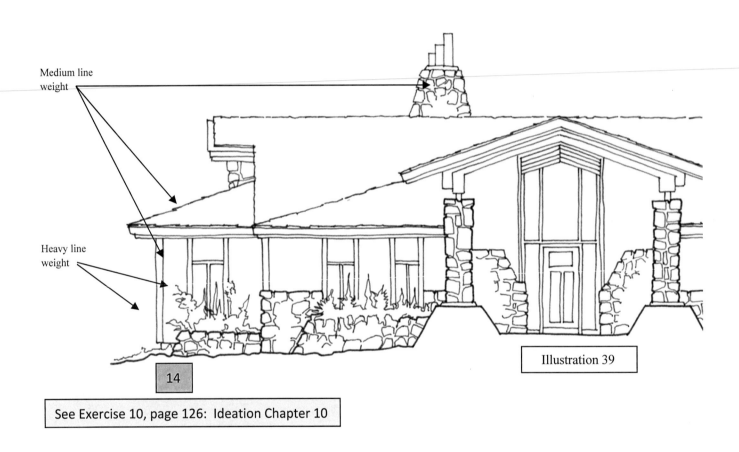

Medium line weight

Heavy line weight

Illustration 39

14

See Exercise 10, page 126: Ideation Chapter 10

Topics covered in Ideation Chapter 4

3-dimensional pictorials:

One-point perspectives

Two-point perspectives

"Birds-eye" illustrations

Furniture detailing: isometric illustrations

Millwork and construction component detailing

One-point perspectives

Chapter 3 conveyed a basic understanding of two and three dimensional illustrations using *"grid scaling"* techniques to assist the designer in setting up basic proportional spatial components and features. With this understanding, Chapter 4 will enhance one's 3-dimensional illustration technique with a more in-depth instruction approach in creating (1) *one and two-point* perspective drawings, (2) isometric drawings, and (3) a unique visual illustration termed as the *"birds-eye"* view also using traditional drafting/sketching methods. Then, one can take these techniques and apply them to concept study drawings used in the design process.

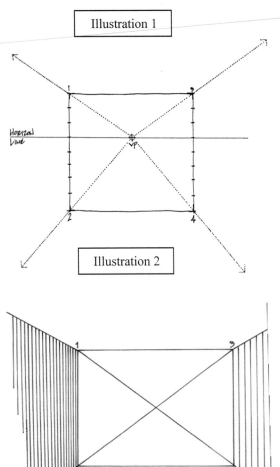

Illustration 1

Illustration 2

Placement of the vanishing point "VP" on horizon line will determine side wall emphasis:

-In Illustration 1, the "VP" is centered on the horizon line, thus giving **equal** emphasis to both side walls, as in Illustration 2.
-In Illustration 3, the "VP" is located to the left of center on the horizon line, giving emphasis to the right wall, creating more visual attention to the wall (Illustration 4).

Note: If the left wall needs to be emphasized more, then the "VP" needs to be located to the right of center on the horizon line.

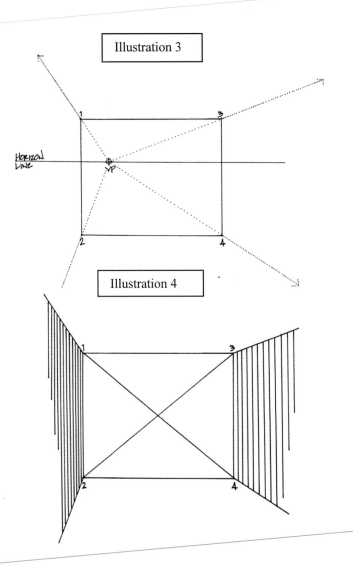

Illustration 3

Illustration 4

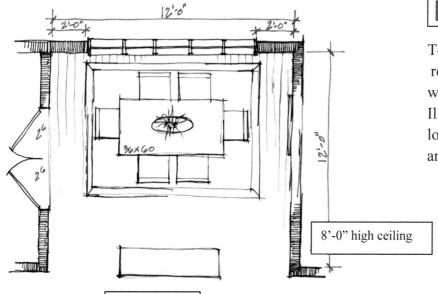

12'-0"

2'-0"   2'-0"

12'-0"

36x60

8'-0" high ceiling

Illustration 5

To help illustrate a *one-point* perspective sketch layout, the dining room floor plan, pictured left (Illustration 5), is used. The back window wall is 12'-0" wide X 8'-0" high drawn below in Illustration 6 with the *center point* of the wall, "VP"/"DP," located. The horizon line estimated at 5'-6" above the floor line and "VP" 2'-6" from line 1-2.

Drawing a vertical line "AB" through the center point of the wall, one can locate "C" and "D," representing the center of the floor and ceiling respectively. This is achieved by extending a line from "DP" through corner point "4" and through "VP" and "B" point "C". Extending a vertical line from "C" toward the ceiling, and a line from "VP" through point "A" to intersect this vertical locate point "D," the center of the ceiling for the space. *Again, all the drawing reference lines are constructed visual "eye-balling" dimensions provided.* This is a technique one should keep practicing to be skilled at doing quickly.

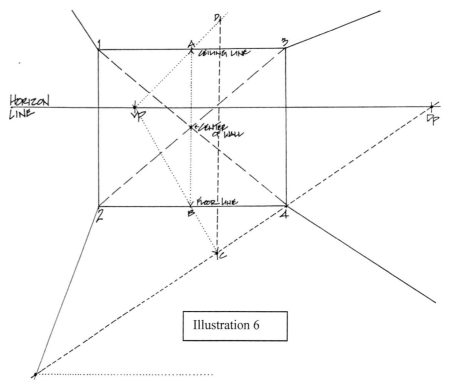

HORIZON LINE

CEILING LINE

CENTER OF WALL

FLOOR LINE

VP

DP

Illustration 6

45

One can lay a piece of trace paper over the previous Illustration 6 to eliminate the reference lines to not be visually complicated in order to start "blocking in" furnishings and interior detailing. The major piece of furniture is the dining table, 4'-0" from the window wall and 5'-0" long, which is located on the floor plane. One should locate all furniture pieces on the floor first as a two-dimensional shape at first, as indicated by the diagonal lines as indicated in Illustration 7.

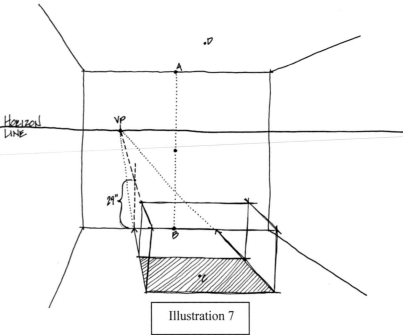

Illustration 7

Sketch vertical lines from each corner of the table plan on the floor, and project a line back to the floor line at back wall as indicated by either arrow, with a vertical line up from that point to "eye-ball" the table height. Then at the estimated 29 inches of table height on the back wall, project a line from "VP" into the space crossing the vertical lines from the two left table corners on the floor. Now, the table height is determined in the room space. Then, with sketched horizontal lines from the intersected lines just drawn across to intersect the **right** vertical lines of floor table corners, the table box is completed. As in Illustration 8, one can box in the chairs and some of the features of the walls using "VP."

See Exercise 11, page 127: Ideation Chapter 10

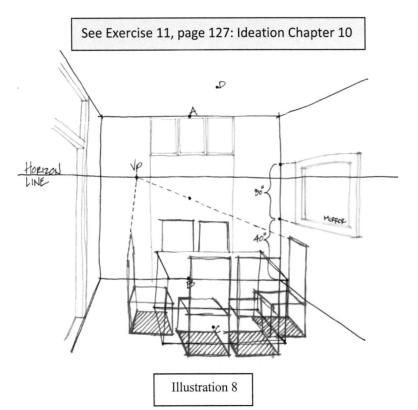

Illustration 8

46

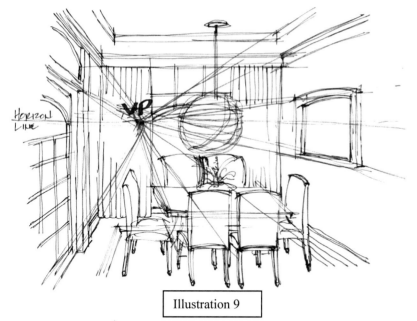

Illustration 9

Illustration 9 shows the various feature detailing for an initial concept sketch with limited surface delineation enhancements, such as floor boards, area rug design lines, drapery lines, door divisions, *trey* ceiling design, and centered ceiling light fixture. Always remember to check yourself with the "VP" to make sure all line work has **perspective correctness,** especially illustrating the ceiling light fixture lines above and below the "VP" and correctly curved to help convey the roundness of the light fixture.

It is important to address "thickness" of all furniture components and interior architectural details, such as chair legs, the picture frame, and door framing/glass division framing.

Illustration 10

Illustration 10 shows the finishes sketch with **"darkened"** edge lines closest to the viewer, such as the foreground chairs, table edge, door divisions, and ceiling light fixture.

Illustration 11 shows a similar space layout with color accents on yellow trace paper to be discussed in Ideation Chapter 5.

Illustration 11

See Exercise 12, page 128: Ideation Chapter 10

Two-point perspectives

In setting up some reference lines for a two-point perspective, first determine the **"true corner"** of the room or space, such as line 1-2 in Illustration 12. Line 3-4 could be chosen instead, but the author chose **1-2** for instruction. Line **1-2** is divided into *eight* segments to represent the ceiling height of 8'-0."

VPL (vanishing point left) was located to the right of true corner line **1-2**, so the left wall, when drawn will be illustrated to the left of line **1-2**. **VPR** (vanishing point right) is located to the far right in order to keep the sketch in a more realistic proportion.

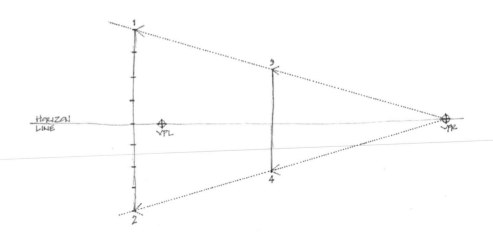

Illustration 12

In Illustration 13, **VPL** is located to the left of true corner line **1-2**, this variation will emphasize the wall from an "outside" of the space view, thus has the potential to block some of the room features. But, the floor and ceiling line on this wall could just be indicated by a solid line and not show any wall detailing. This technique is known as "ghosting" in, so the viewer is looking through the wall seeing inside the room, *just like "Superman" can see through a wall.*

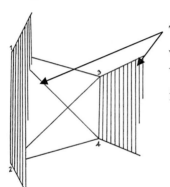

This sketch shows walls that would be emphasized using VPL "option" & VPR locations indicated in Illustration 13.

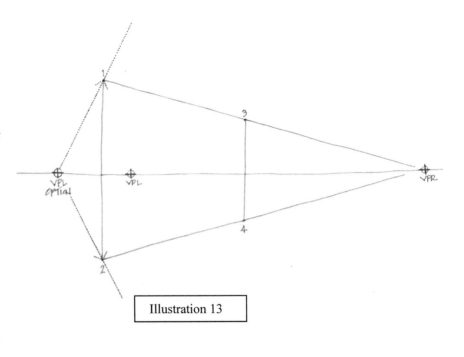

Illustration 13

48

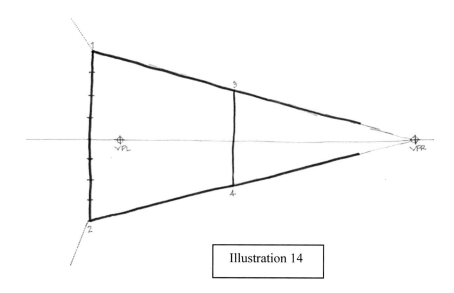

Illustration 14

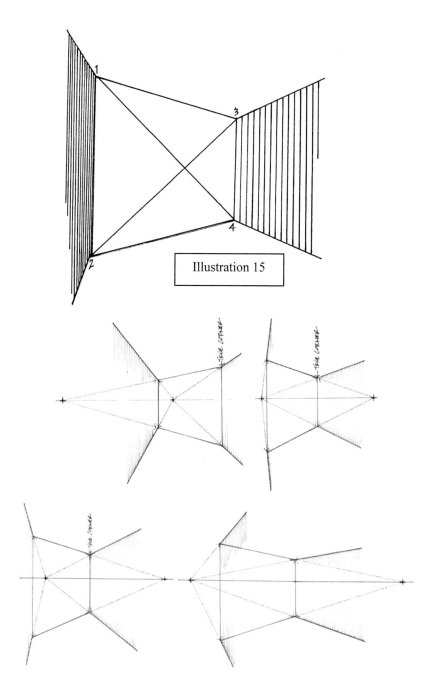

Illustration 15

Illustration 14 shows **VPL** to the right of the true corner line 1-2, that emphasizes the inside surface of the left wall which changed the view of the orientation emphasis of the wall from "outside" of the space as shown in Illustration 13.

Now, one can visually compare the wall emphasis between Illustration 13 and its companion sketch with Illustration 14 and 15 to determine the desired wall orientation for a project.

As another view orientation option needing to emphasize the "outside" surface of the *right wall* instead, just designate line 3-4 as the "true corner" and move **VPR** closer to line 3-4 and **VPL** more to the left. (Experiment, moving VPL and VPR along the horizon line to visualize the various allocations of all three walls as shown in the multiple views to the right).

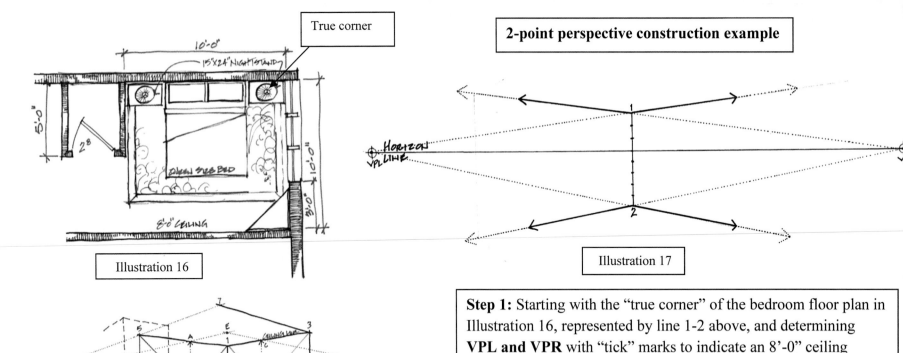

True corner

Illustration 16

Illustration 17

Illustration 19

Step 1: Starting with the "true corner" of the bedroom floor plan in Illustration 16, represented by line 1-2 above, and determining **VPL and VPR** with "tick" marks to indicate an 8'-0" ceiling height, the initial floor and ceiling lines can be drawn. *VPL draws lines to the right and VPR draws lines to the left within a sketch.*

Illustration 18

Step 2: "Eye-ball" the two major wall surface sizes (10'-0" lengths) as depicted in "Illustration 18" and the small 5'-0" deep closet, then check the perspective "correctness" of line work with **VPL and VPR**.

Next, for *future reference*, find the major wall center points, drawing lines from corner-to-corner as indicated in Illustration 19. **Note: extending lines from both vanishing points through "A" and "C" will locate the ceiling center "E."**

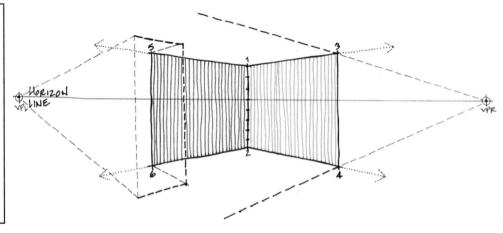

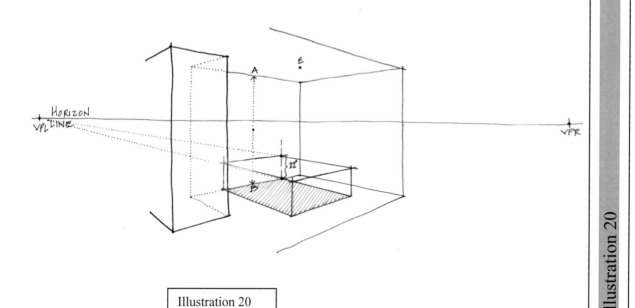

Illustration 20

Step 3: Blocking in furniture pieces:

-locate the bed size on the floor, back of bed against the wall, and project vertical lines from each corner on the floor

-choose one of those vertical lines against the wall and "eyeball" a 22" height for the bed

-project a line from **VPL** out into the room to where the line intersects the vertical from the bed corner and finish the bed block maneuvering lines from both vanishing points

After locating the night stands and triangular corner furniture piece, checking lines of perspective correctness, the window and door can be located as depicted.

-the 30" height for the corner furniture piece is located by projecting a line from a "tick" mark from the original true corner across the window wall as shown

-the two night stands (22" height) are located using the same procedure, projecting the guide lines from either vanishing point

Illustration 21

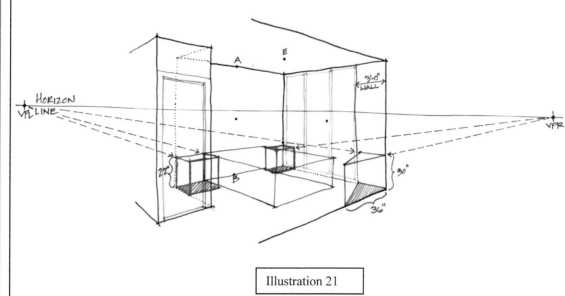

Illustration 21

51

Step 4: Add detailing enhancements

-conveyed in the illustration is the picture on the wall, door handle, recessed ceiling/light can, area rug, bed pillows and spread, *rounding the bed end corners will soften the "box" mattresses.*

-the furnishings "dotted" in are obviously not seen due to the locations of VPL and VPR, but it is beneficial to lightly block in all furnishings and components just to verify the items that are viewed in relation to perspective correctness.

Always verify perspective correctness with the vanishing points as shown.

Illustration 22

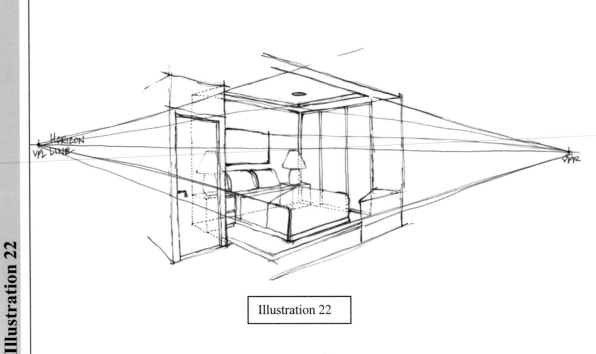

Illustration 22

Illustration 23, the sketch shown with erased construction guidelines and additional graphic line enhancements for the artwork, bed ruffles, and area rug as a more finished presentation concept drawing. All line work now is done with a black felt-tip design pen.

But, one can choose to leave all construction line for a more "loose/concept" look to the sketch.

See Exercise 13, page 129: Ideation Chapter 10, then complete Exercise 14, page 130

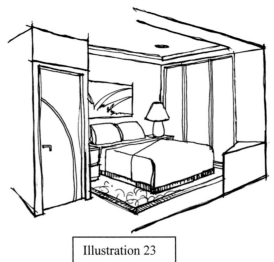

Illustration 23

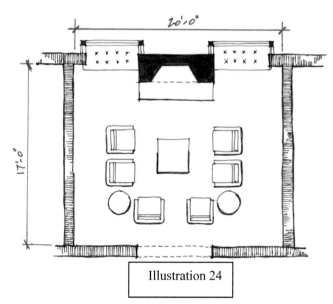

Illustration 24

The "bird's-eye" illustration technique is a unique type of visual drawing. The orientation looking down into a space from an above viewpoint will obviously emphasize the walls and it's features, and the floor. For this illustration example Illustration 24 will be used, and the ceiling height will be 9'-0."

This type of illustration is created by using the **one-point** perspective construction drawing technique and locating the **VP** in the center of the space as shown in Illustration 25.

Step 1: Drawing a line from **VP** to each corner of the room and extending those lines beyond begin to form the walls of the space.

Step 2: Find the wall height by locating the **DP,** or "diagonal point" on the horizon line. The **DP** is the distance one is viewing the illustration from above the room/space, and measured to either the right or left of the **VP**. In this illustration, the author has chosen the **DP** to the right as shown.

Step 3: The long dashed line from **DP** through corner number 4 and extended to intersect the solid line 9'-0" from corner number 4 drawn from **VP** determines the wall height.

Illustration 25

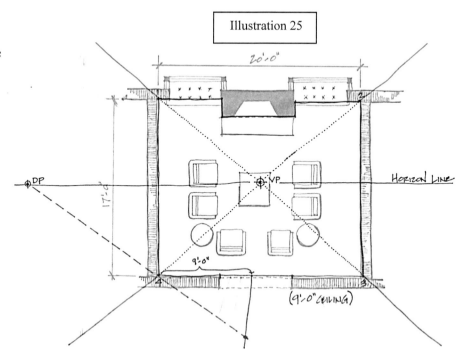

53

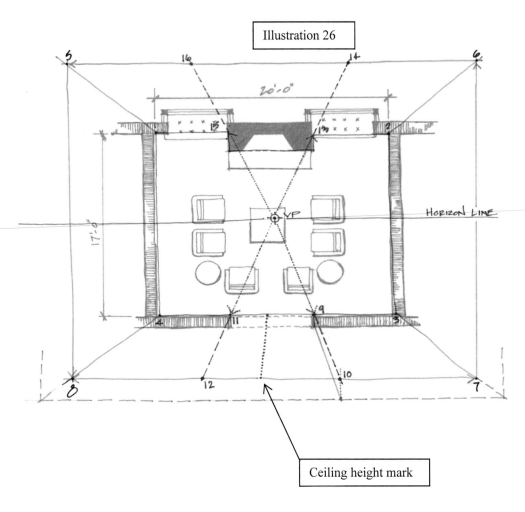

Illustration 26

20'-0"

17'-0"

HORIZON LINE

VP

Ceiling height mark

Similar projected lines from corner points on the plan intersecting the top wall lines will start to define various feature elements, doorways, and windows of the plan *(illustrated through points "11-12", "13-14", and "15-16".*

Step 4: A horizontal line through the ceiling height mark just created in Step 3 will define the top of wall line "7-8," then one can finish all wall line tops by completing the "box" indicated by the intersection of lines drawn from each floor corner of the room from **VP** *(illustrated through points 5, 6, 7, and 8).*

Step 5: Now, a line from **VP** through point 9 that intersects line "7-8" and creates point "10" is one of the doorway opening corners indicated by the dashed lines "9-10" and "11-12."

Step 6: (Wall thickness) Project a line from **VP** through the door opening corner opposite point "9." Drop a vertical line from point "10" to where the line intersects the corner line just drawn and that intersection point is the *dashed* line drawn horizontally, which creates the wall thickness. Extended lines through points "7" and "8" that intersect the horizontal *dashed* line will now define vertical wall thicknesses left and right.

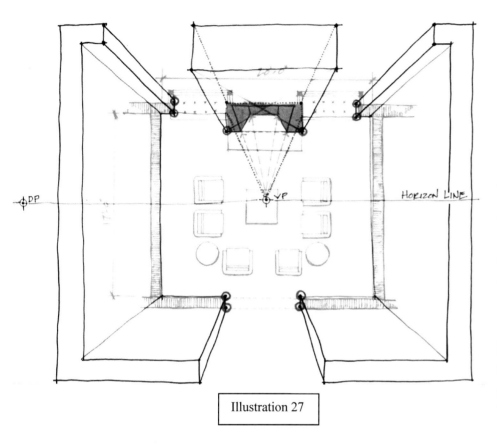

See Exercise 15, page 131, Ideation Chapter 10

Illustration 27

Step 7: (Architectural features) Project lines from VP through the circled points up to the top of the wall thicknesses that define the doorway and window cased openings as conveyed in "Illustration 27."

Step 8: (Fireplace) Project lines from VP through the circled points at fireplace corners and the back two corners of the fireplace (indicated by the shaded plan area of the fireplace). The projected dotted lines intersecting the exterior top wall line, one can drop two short vertical lines down into the illustration to where they intersect the projected lines through the **circled** points of the fireplace front corners. Now, the top fireplace thickness is created.

Step 9: (Fireplace opening) The projected dashed lines through the four points of the fireplace opening of the shaded plan of the fireplace create the opening width. Then, "eye-balling" a height of 4'-0" for the opening, draw a horizontal line. Two back lines of the firebox shape stop at this horizontal line.

Step 10: (Blocking in the furniture) Each furniture piece on the plan is three-dimensionally drawn using the **VP** projection methods just like creating one and two-point perspectives discussed previously. "Illustration 28" to the right has each furniture piece cross-hatched to be created three-dimensionally. Project lines from **VP** through each corner of the two left chairs, and to locate the height of the chair back, project a line (**dashed**) from the back corner of chair to the wall- "line 4-5." Where that line hits the inside line of the wall, project a dashed up the wall as shown. "Eye-ball" a 3'-0" measurement from the left room corner along the wall base and project a line (3) (**dotted**) up the wall from **VP**. Now, a line (**dashed**) from **DP point** on horizon line through the left room corner across the wall and intersects with line (3).

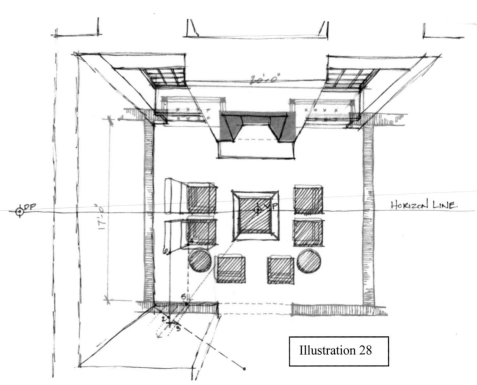

Illustration 28

Step 11: (Furniture heights) The intersection of **line 3/point 3,** draw a short horizontal line to intersect the dashed line up the wall previously drawn. This will locate the chair back height to project a vertical (**solid**) line back into the room space to intersect the line from the bottom left corner plan of the chair from **VP**.

Then "eye-ball" a chair back thickness. This process will then let the designer to further "eye-ball" seat heights, table heights since one has a reference furniture piece drawn to complete all other furnishings.

Illustration 29 to the left shows the finished free-hand sketch.

See Exercise 16, page132: Ideation Chapter 10

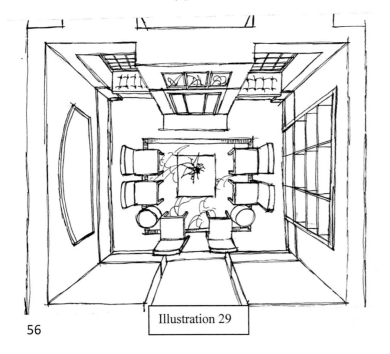

Illustration 29

Furniture detail sketching

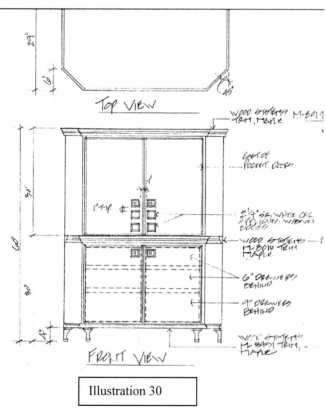

Top View

Front View

Illustration 30

Step 1: Furniture sketches can be easily conveyed by using isometric drawing techniques, since again, one can measure distances on all constructed guidelines. The TV armoire depicted in Illustration 30 first is blocking in of the overall size of the unit with the few quick measurements (indicated) to scale. Then, "eye-balling" features such as the base legs and angled corners.

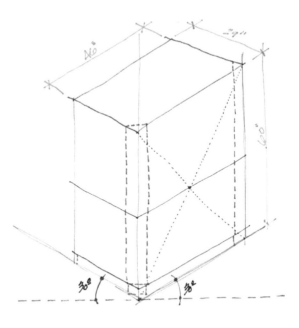

Step 2: With lightly sketched guidelines, draw in the unit's detail lines/features.

Step 3: Go back over with a black felt tip pen to create a more refined look to the sketch.

See Exercise 17, page 133: Ideation Chapter 10, then, complete Exercise 18, page 134

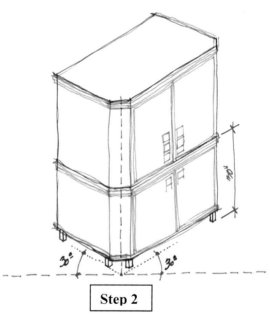

Step 3

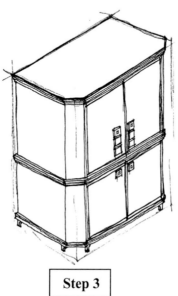

Step 2

Chair design and sketching in the interior design profession is a constant significant furniture piece to illustrate, not only as a single piece, but multiple illustrations of the same piece. The chair, in the grouping of three in Illustration 31 obviously has (3) various views, with a slightly different orientation. So, it is important for the designer to understand the components of the piece visually as one illustrates the chair in multiple views.

Illustration 31

Using the same steps as illustrated on the previous page for the TV armoire, the overall chair size is blocked, seat height is determined, and the lines of the legs are indicated in the left sketch below. Then, sketching in the "rolled" back and waterfall seat front edge, and the curving of the seat and back give the chair a more soft ergonomic perspective in the middle sketch below. Adding thickness to the back, seat, and legs creates the true realistic view. *Creating "thickness" in sketching is so important for visual depth in any sketch.*

Finished felt-tip line sketch

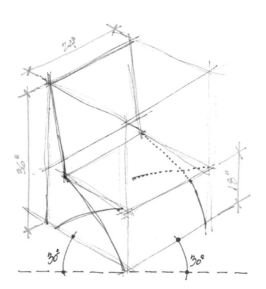

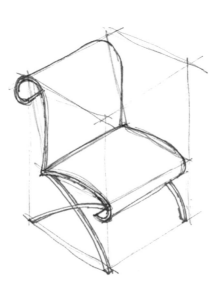

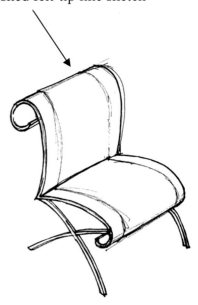

Sometimes, it is more visually appealing to create the sketch using the two-point perspective technique, especially if one is illustrating the furniture pieces in a room setting environment.

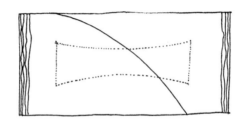

Experience has shown that isometric sketching is appropriate for illustrating individual furnishing pieces.

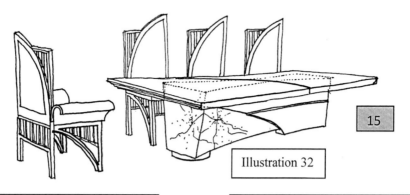

15

Illustration 32

Step 1: Block in the overall rectilinear shape of the dining table in "Illustration 32", locating a ***true corner*** below the horizon line to show the top of the table. Use the "eye-balling" technique for determining distances.

Step 2: As indicated with the guide lines below, draw in the various design details of the table. Once satisfied with the feature detailing proportions, then one can go over the line work with a black felt-tip to create a finished version as above.

See Exercise 19, page 135: Ideation Chapter 10

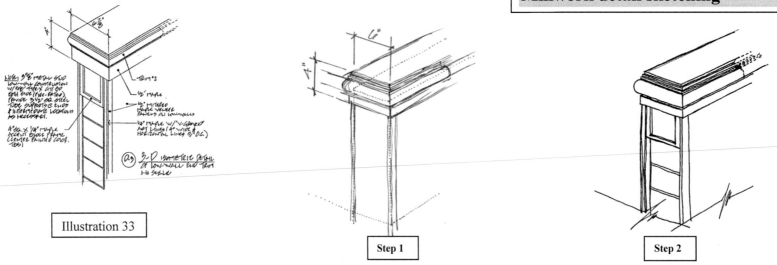

Illustration 33

Step 1

Step 2

If the designer is asked to quickly sketch some ideas for millwork detailing, then the isometric drawing is the author's choice. Again, one can easily measure a few reference dimensions on the isometric construction guidelines for detail accuracy and finish the sketch in minutes. By now, throughout all of the sketching illustrations presented in this chapter, the important message is to always "block in" the overall detail shape as depicted in Step 1 of Illustrations 33/34 to ultimately create the more finished sketches in Step 2.

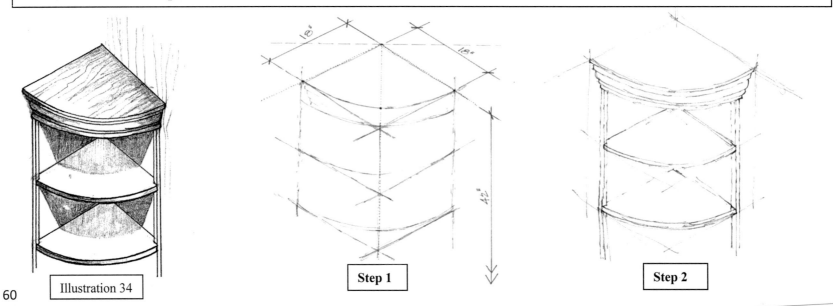

Illustration 34

Step 1

Step 2

Isometric sketches are also appropriate for a millwork detail conveyed in Illustration 35 to depict construction components in **cross-section** to the right of the thickened black line, then showing those components pictorially to the left of thickened black line on the true 30-degree line for the isometric. The thickened black line is a technique to incorporate in distinguishing construction components in **cross-section** and adds visual line variety to the preliminary concept sketch prior to CAD documentation.

"Illustrations 36/37/38" below are standard types of 2-dimensional sketches for various millwork concept sketches designers frequently need to address throughout the design process, investigating detailing synthesis. Chapter 8 will further provide additional finished examples of various millwork detailing.

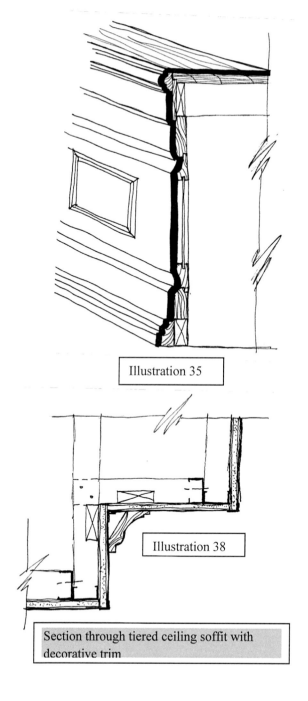

Illustration 35

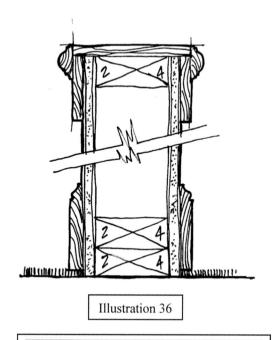

Illustration 36

Vertical section through wood-capped, low partition

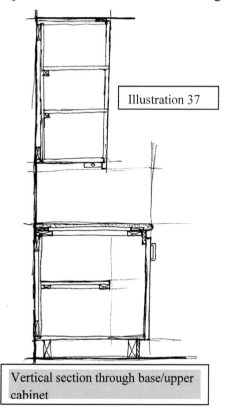

Illustration 37

Illustration 38

Vertical section through base/upper cabinet

Section through tiered ceiling soffit with decorative trim

Topics covered in Ideation Chapter 5

Delineation enhancements:

Material "surfacing"

Materials in "section"

Scaling detail

Light sources and feature accent highlighting

Quick color, why not?

Delineations: Within the design disciplines, the visual enhancement using graphic line work on surfaces and in section cuts through construction component detailing to convey the textural, hardness and softness, and pattern of various finish materials is an important skill to development and understand. It is an illustrative technique that one should begin to develop insight as to the **"level of scale"** the delineation would be most appropriate for the type drawing and it's scale being conveyed. Various levels of scale range in the amount of detail needed on material "surfacing" and "sections" of the drawing, from floor plans, elevations, 3-dimensional illustrations to building construction components and furnishing illustrations. The intent of Ideation Chapter 5 is share some standard delineation graphics for various types of drawings a designer would use in hand-sketched concept illustrations in the design process. These delineations are also a part of the computer-aided software menu selections.

Material "surfacing"

The following surface delineation graphics are representative of design industry standards illustrated at approximately 3/4" = 1'-0" scale. Standard delineations are typically depicted for wood, concrete, glass, carpet, marble/granite, ceramic tile, stone, concrete block, and brick.

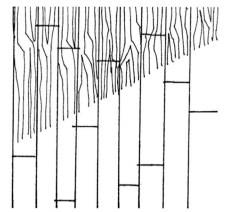

- 3" wide plank flooring
- Wood graining using a "rigid" line graphic illustrated to a light pencil guideline (not visually overwhelming)

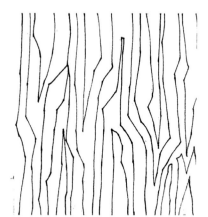

- Wood graining close-up
- Delineation could be used on wall elevations and furniture pieces

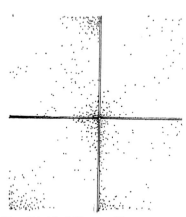

- Divided ("scored") concrete
- "Stippling" technique used with point of felt tip concentrating from corners out

Sometimes it may be visually beneficial to not delineate the whole surface, so not to be "visually overwhelming," too busy. Further visual explanations are depicted on drawings later in this chapter on **"scaling detailing."**

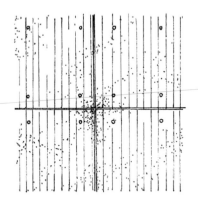

■Pre-cast "ribbed" concrete panels
■Used on wall elevations with "form" holes and "stippling" technique

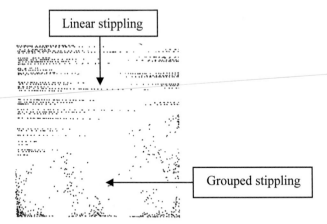

Linear stippling

Grouped stippling

■ Two variations of carpet delineations
■ "Stippling" technique used

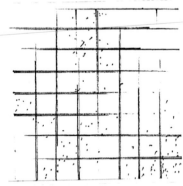

■Floor tile delineation
■Double lines for grouting and sporadic "stippling" technique

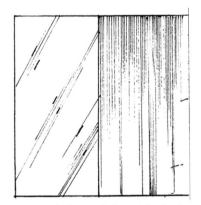

■Two variations of glass (glazing)
■60-degree lines with small dark accent dashes or vertical lines

Groups of intersecting grain lines with concentrated stippling

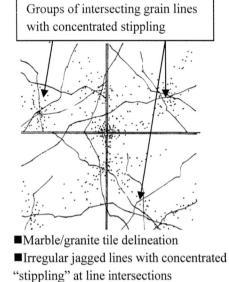

■Marble/granite tile delineation
■Irregular jagged lines with concentrated "stippling" at line intersections

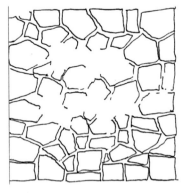

■Stone paver delineation
■Large/small stones with broken line area

The technique of "broken line" areas as depicted on the previous page and this page simply is done to reduce the complexity and overstimulation of the illustration. In addition, the broken line areas gives a sense of light sources hitting the surface and the fading out of some of the finish material line divisions and the material itself as natural and artificial light phenomena happens within and outside of living environment spaces.

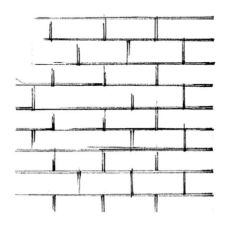

■ Uniform linear width stone pattern
with broken lines
■ Show variety of shapes/lengths

■ Concrete block pattern
(standard nominal size: 8 X 8 X 16)
■Double grouting lines at this scale

■ Standard "running bond" brick
(standard nominal size: 3 X 4 X 8)
■Double grouting lines at this scale

Note: indicating "double lines" for masonry units (stone/concrete block/brick) is visually readable at drawing scales 3/8" = 1'-0" and larger. Less than 3/8" = 1'-0" scale, single line work for grouting spacing is sufficient so not to be too visually complex because the architectural and interior construction features are the most important. Do not overpower the illustration with delineation techniques. This topic is covered in **"scaling detailing"** and Ideation Chapter 7 "When is enough, enough?"

See Exercise 20, page 136: Ideation Chapter 10

Materials in section

When a material such as a "slab" of marble or granite is broken or saw-cut and is viewed along that edge, the term for that edge cut view is a *material in section*. Some delineation can be illustrated both as a "surface" or "section" graphic representation. The following sketches illustrate *materials in section* through a cut/broken edge:

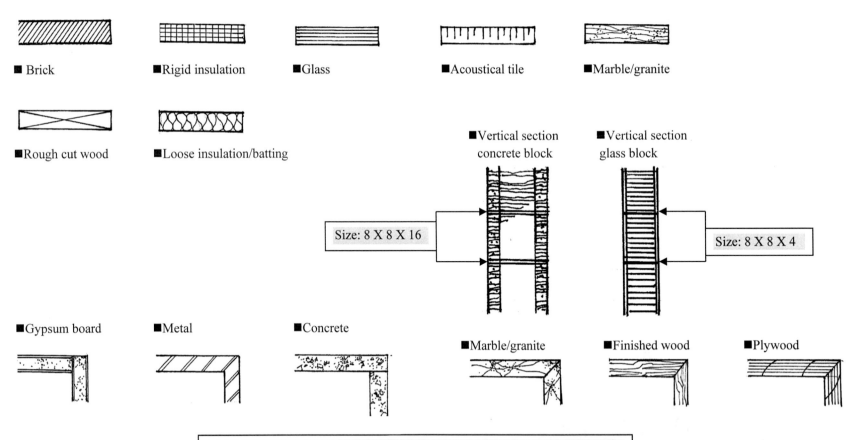

■ Brick   ■Rigid insulation   ■Glass   ■Acoustical tile   ■Marble/granite

■Rough cut wood   ■Loose insulation/batting

■Vertical section concrete block   ■Vertical section glass block

Size: 8 X 8 X 16

Size: 8 X 8 X 4

■Gypsum board   ■Metal   ■Concrete

■Marble/granite   ■Finished wood   ■Plywood

These illustrations of "corner" connections for various materials could represent wall and/or furniture surface cladding over constructed framing.

Process drawings can include various interior partition/millwork detailing to assist the designer in conceptualizing how these built interior components will actually be constructed. And, hand sketched details will help in the preparation of final CAD-generated construction documents. The knowledge of construction components and materials, industry standard sizes, and their material delineation graphic illustrations will help insure the intended understanding of the detail to the viewer. And, hand sketched versions could eliminate future discrepancies and changes during the design development and construction document phase. *Ideation Chapter 8* will share developed detailing examples that include dimensions and construction notes, and graphic title information.

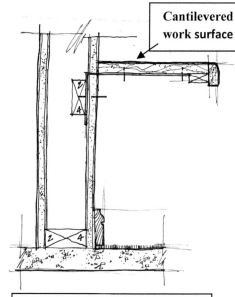

Cantilevered work surface

2 x 4 wood stud interior partition, "vertical" section on concrete slab with cantilevered work surface line sketch

2 X 4 wood stud interior partition, "vertical "section with construction material delineations

Window glazing/glass with wood jamb and "stops"

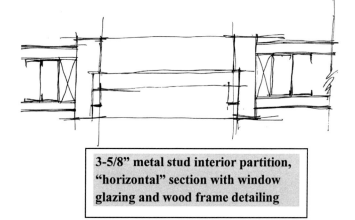

3-5/8" metal stud interior partition, "horizontal" section with window glazing and wood frame detailing

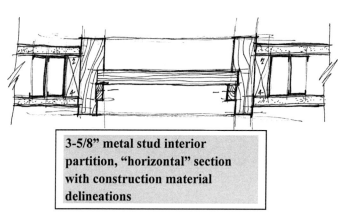

3-5/8" metal stud interior partition, "horizontal" section with construction material delineations

Example below of a furniture leg and top detail sketch using the "blocking" technique to identify spatial size of construction components. **Note:** Preliminary construction detailing "thinking" is typically hand-sketched at *no scale*.

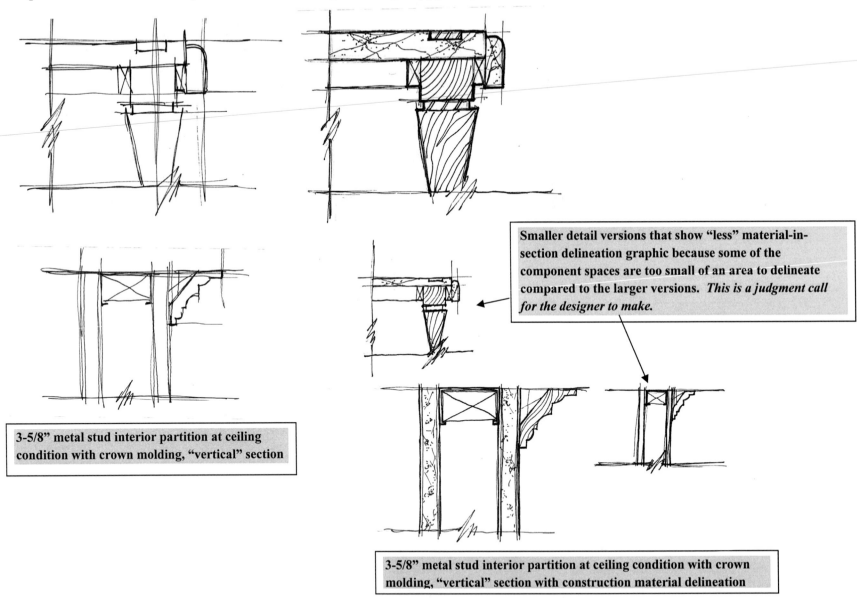

Smaller detail versions that show "less" material-in-section delineation graphic because some of the component spaces are too small of an area to delineate compared to the larger versions. *This is a judgment call for the designer to make.*

3-5/8" metal stud interior partition at ceiling condition with crown molding, "vertical" section

3-5/8" metal stud interior partition at ceiling condition with crown molding, "vertical" section with construction material delineation

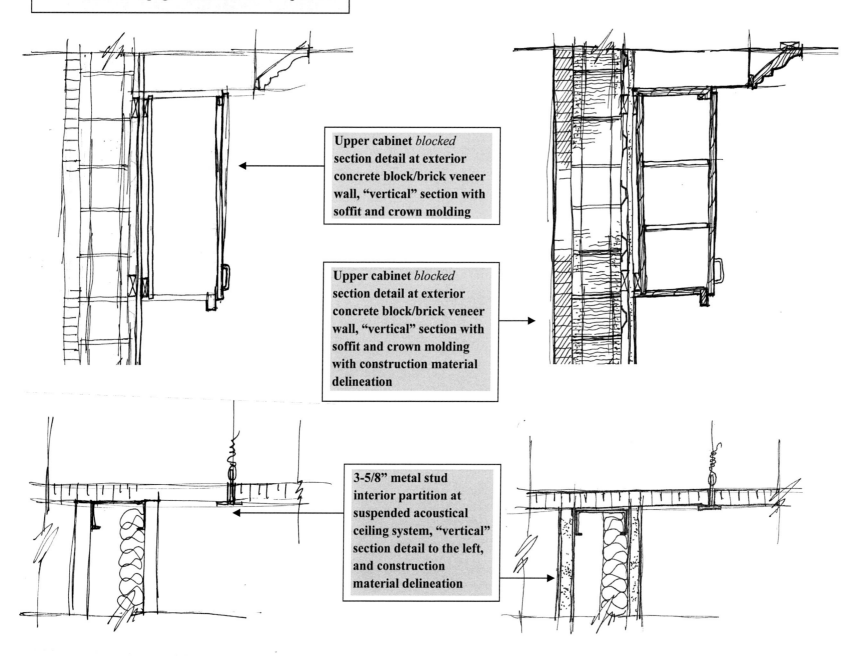

See Exercise 21, page 137: Ideation Chapter 10

Upper cabinet *blocked* section detail at exterior concrete block/brick veneer wall, "vertical" section with soffit and crown molding

Upper cabinet *blocked* section detail at exterior concrete block/brick veneer wall, "vertical" section with soffit and crown molding with construction material delineation

3-5/8" metal stud interior partition at suspended acoustical ceiling system, "vertical" section detail to the left, and construction material delineation

Window treatments are significant illustrations to master in free-hand sketching that sometimes do not get the attention they deserve especially if they are an important feature to the client in the design process. The amount of delineation detail depends on the project design intent and scale of the illustration as is with type of drawing document. The illustrations below are just a few of the many creative variations of window treatments available on the market and the designer's imagination. Applications are depicted later within this chapter.

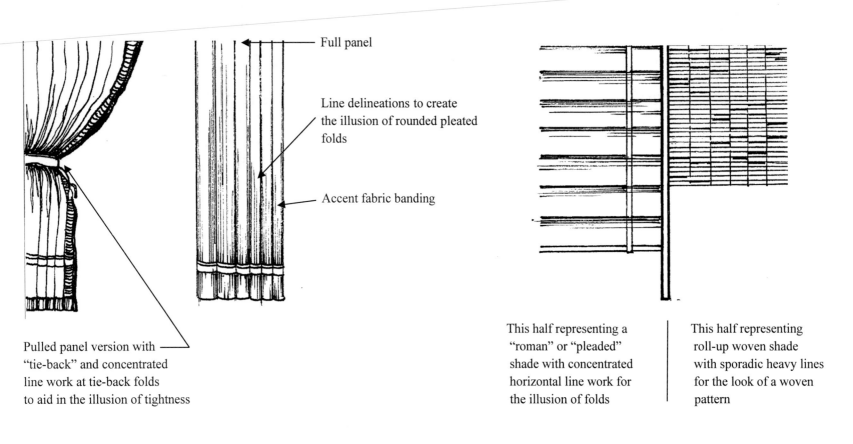

Full panel

Line delineations to create the illusion of rounded pleated folds

Accent fabric banding

Pulled panel version with "tie-back" and concentrated line work at tie-back folds to aid in the illusion of tightness

This half representing a "roman" or "pleated" shade with concentrated horizontal line work for the illusion of folds

This half representing roll-up woven shade with sporadic heavy lines for the look of a woven pattern

See Exercise 22, page 138: Ideation Chapter 10

Applying delineation graphics to illustrate finish materials on 2 and 3-dimensional sketches not only helps to bring "stylistic life" to the drawing, but also, helps convey to the viewer/client a visual sense of the design intent. Delineations convey *pattern, texture, hardness and softness, and scale* to the conceptual sketching process. A partial bedroom sitting area floor plan indicated in Illustration 1 is the basic hand-sketched line drawing to show floor covering options 1, 2, and 3 at a scale of 3/16" = 1'-0".

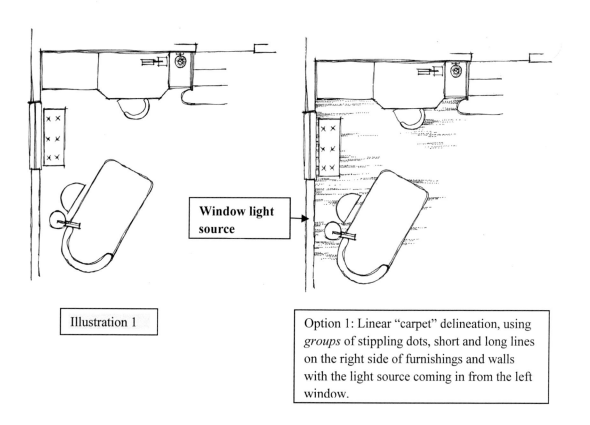

Window light source

Illustration 1

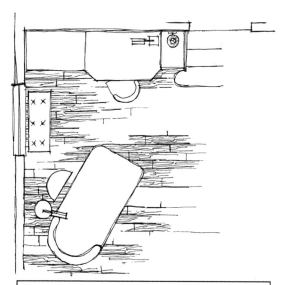

Option 1: Linear "carpet" delineation, using *groups* of stippling dots, short and long lines on the right side of furnishings and walls with the light source coming in from the left window.

Option 2: 4" wide wood plank flooring with using *groups* of graining delineation, fading into room area towards the right.

Option 3 is illustrated on the next page.

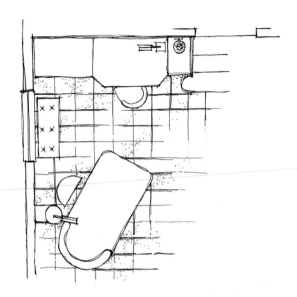

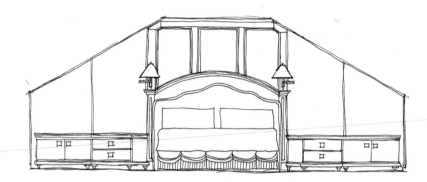

Illustration 2: Bedroom interior wall elevation, hand-sketched with final black felt tip line work.

Option 3: 8" X 8" ceramic tile flooring *groups* of stippling delineation and areas of faded tile double lines for grout widths.

Option 1: faded wood grain delineation

Window glazing with vertical line work

Option 2: wood grain delineation taken to an "imaginary" light guide line

NOTE: Depending on the need for the complexity of the visual communication, the designer may need to illustrate the material delineation to fill or nearly fill the space allocated to convey to the viewer, especially if a particular pattern or grain direction is to be conveyed.

See Exercise 23, page 139: Ideation Chapter 10

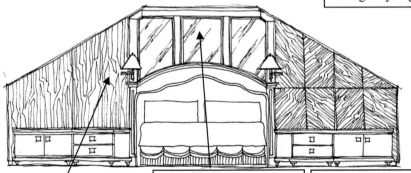

Option 3: full wood grain delineation on both panels

Window glazing with 45-degree grouped lines, some with heavy accent dashes

Option 4: full wood grain delineation to show "pattern"

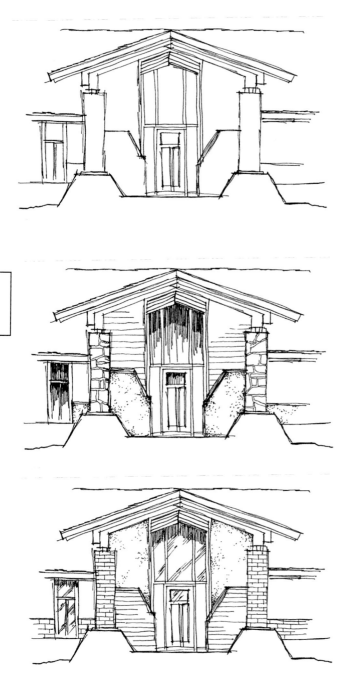

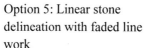

Option 5: Linear stone delineation with faded line work

Stippled dot delineation to represent painted wall surface

Option 6: Irregular "field" stone delineation

See Exercise 24, page 140: Ideation Chapter 10

Illustration 4: The exterior elevations to the right, beginning with the hand-sketched "line" version and two material surface delineation illustrations show the same type of techniques as seen in the interior elevation examples. In illustrating exterior elevations of 3-dimensional perspective views, it is so important to stress depth on the window glazing with "shadow" from overhangs. The two illustrations to the right have *close* vertical delineated lines to create the shadow depth. Not shown, is the shadow on the wall surfaces so to stress the window glazing for the examples.

The hand-sketched 3-dimensional interior concept illustrations are usually the most preferred to fully convey the design process thinking. Designers should develop a skill level they are comfortable with for perspective sketching to convey their ideas in a visually appealing format that is clear to the viewer, clean in appearance (not so free-hand that appears as sloppy work). Sure, guidelines can be left on the sketch, but having a finalized sketch with darkened line work, such as using felt-tip pens in varying line weights portrays professionalism, crispness to the sketch, and a drawing that can be shared with various viewers and project documentation.

The following 3-D sketch illustrations address the initial "blocking" technique line work to create the drawing, but also, material surface delineations that can enhance and further illustrate the design intent.

Illustration 5: Corporate office lobby sketch with preliminary pencil guidelines erased and finalized felt-tip line work.

Ceiling soffit

Option 1: Linear carpet and stipple dots for flooring, marble sheet delineation for lower ceiling soffit, "formed" concrete panels with faded vertical line work/stippling, and office window glazing.

Option 2: Marble and linear carpet flooring delineations, wood graining on office door, marble wall panels, office window glazing, and stippling for painted ceiling and soffit.

Illustration 6: Resort cabin retreat living space sketch with preliminary pencil guidelines erased and finalized felt-tip line work.

Flat screen TV

Option 1: Field stone flooring, linear stone fireplace structure with field stone hearth/wood trim board, upper wood grain delineation around flat screen TV, concrete fireplace mantle, wood slat ceiling/side wall/upper fireplace feature, stippled upper wall surfaces, and pleated window treatments.

Option 2: Stippled and "scored" concrete flooring, grain-delineated wood beams/trim, stippled wall/ceiling surfaces, tiled fireplace hearth/wood trim board, concrete fireplace mantle, brick fireplace structure, wood graining on upper fireplace feature, and woven window treatment delineation.

This two-point hand-sketched perspective shows the interior architecture component detailing that conveys enough design intent to the viewer through the various surface delineation techniques discussed previously in the chapter. And, notice the ***fading*** and ***grouping*** of the delineations that help to create "visual surface variation" so not to be too overwhelming.

See Exercise 25, page 141: Ideation Chapter 10, then, complete Exercise 26, page 142

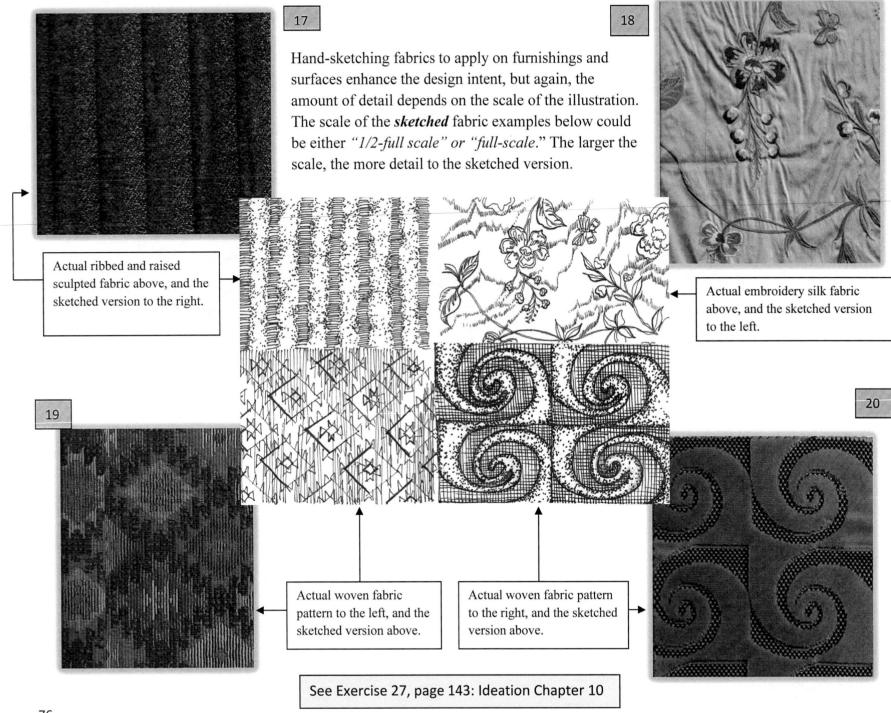

17

Hand-sketching fabrics to apply on furnishings and surfaces enhance the design intent, but again, the amount of detail depends on the scale of the illustration. The scale of the *sketched* fabric examples below could be either *"1/2-full scale"* or *"full-scale."* The larger the scale, the more detail to the sketched version.

18

Actual ribbed and raised sculpted fabric above, and the sketched version to the right.

Actual embroidery silk fabric above, and the sketched version to the left.

19

20

Actual woven fabric pattern to the left, and the sketched version above.

Actual woven fabric pattern to the right, and the sketched version above.

See Exercise 27, page 143: Ideation Chapter 10

76

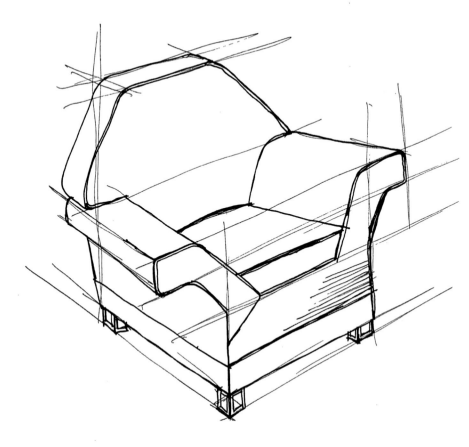

In custom furniture design, the amount and scale of the feature detailing is a significant factor to convey the design intent. The fading of the delineation is appropriate, as long as there is enough to show the fabric pattern and design. Delineated fabrics on the lounge chair below are from the illustrations on the previous page with an additional "alligator" fabric pattern incorporated.

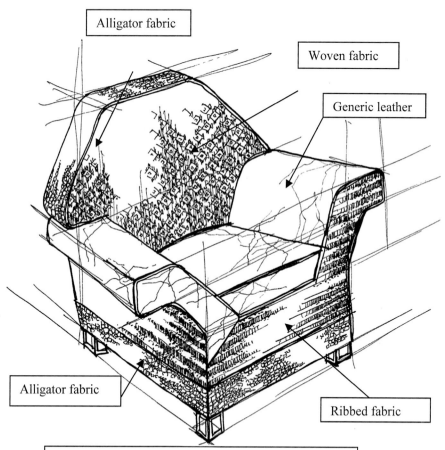

Alligator fabric

Woven fabric

Generic leather

Alligator fabric

Ribbed fabric

Illustration 7: "Blocked" lounge chair, two-point perspective sketch showing double lines to represent welt-cording trim detailing. Notice the rounded corners on arms and seat back to help **"soften"** the feature lines.

See Exercise 28, page 144: Ideation Chapter 10

The upholstery fabric delineations scaled down to fit the size and proportions of the lounge chair feature areas to complement the scale of the "actual" fabric illustrated on the previous page.

77

In hand-sketching furniture pieces, the author has found that either two-point perspectives or isometric views are the best techniques to use for these types of illustrations to portray more of a realistic depiction. And, again leaving or not leaving the blocking guidelines is at the discretion of the designer, depending on how "formal" one wants the illustration to be viewed.

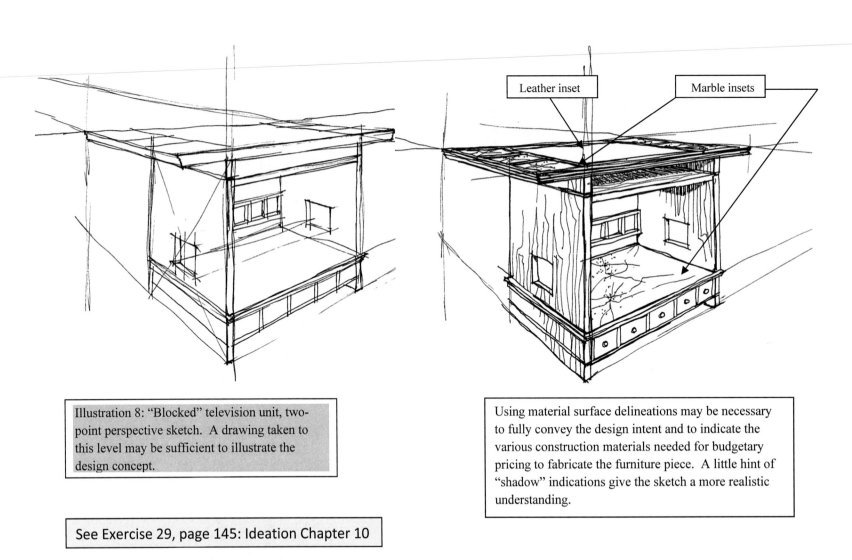

Leather inset

Marble insets

Illustration 8: "Blocked" television unit, two-point perspective sketch. A drawing taken to this level may be sufficient to illustrate the design concept.

Using material surface delineations may be necessary to fully convey the design intent and to indicate the various construction materials needed for budgetary pricing to fabricate the furniture piece. A little hint of "shadow" indications give the sketch a more realistic understanding.

See Exercise 29, page 145: Ideation Chapter 10

Light sources and accent lighting

A number of previous sketches have shown a hint of light sources to enhance the illustration. If the designer's intent of the sketch is to engage the viewer within the interior environment with the furniture pieces(s), the reflecting or non-reflecting value of surface materials, the textural quality of materials, and the hardness or softness of materials, and overall depth of the sketch, ***light sources*** should be determined (the angle/direction of the light source). These light sources can either come through the windows, glass doors, and/or skylights as "natural" light or general illumination from various types of light fixtures within the space. ***Accent light sources*** are light fixtures that direct a specific angle of light onto various "focal points" of intended interest, such as art work, signage, entry areas/doors, task/work surfaces, and highlighting textural wall, ceiling, and floor surfaces. The following illustration examples are simply to convey the impact of "natural" and "accent light" sources can have on the sketch in creating *visual depth, surface illumination highlights, and some "life" animation* to the sketch. These delineation techniques also help define shape and form of the furnishings and interior features through the lighted surfaces, shades, and shadows. The following sketches illustrate various light sources and suggested delineation techniques to convey the highlighted versus shaded areas.

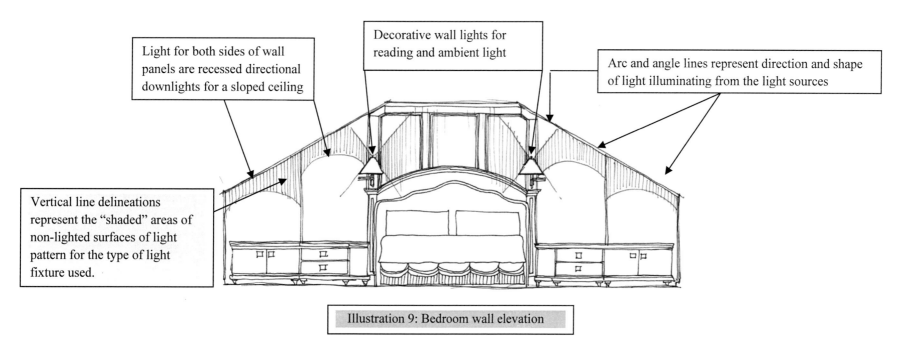

Light for both sides of wall panels are recessed directional downlights for a sloped ceiling

Decorative wall lights for reading and ambient light

Arc and angle lines represent direction and shape of light illuminating from the light sources

Vertical line delineations represent the "shaded" areas of non-lighted surfaces of light pattern for the type of light fixture used.

Illustration 9: Bedroom wall elevation

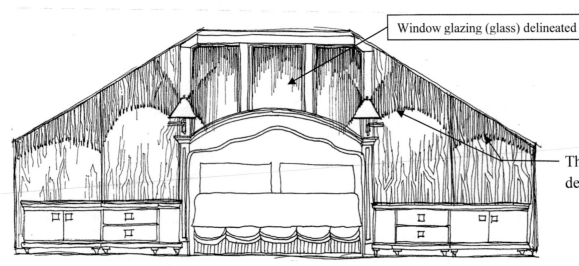

Window glazing (glass) delineated

The small heavy/tight lines segments help define the non-lighted surfaces.

Option delineation 1: Series of vertical lines to show *"lighted" and "non-lighted"* areas based on light source definitions in "Illustration 9" on the previous page.

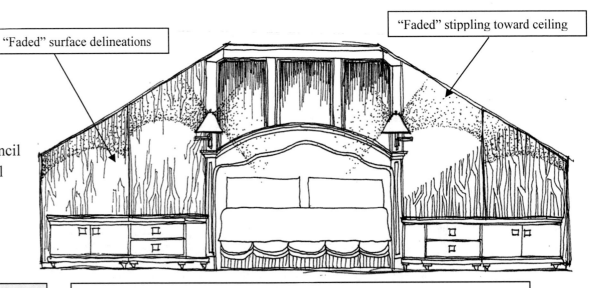

"Faded" stippling toward ceiling

"Faded" surface delineations

Again, these illustrations have had their pencil guidelines removed for a more refined final sketch.

See Exercise 30, page 146: Ideation Chapter 10

Option delineation 2: Stippling delineation over surface material delineation to show *"lighted and non-lighted" areas*

Dropped ceiling soffit and acoustical tile plane with recessed down lights to accent the directory and concrete panel surface texture using vertical line delineations over panels.

Suspended ceiling pendant light fixtures and recessed light sources above art and fireplace opening.

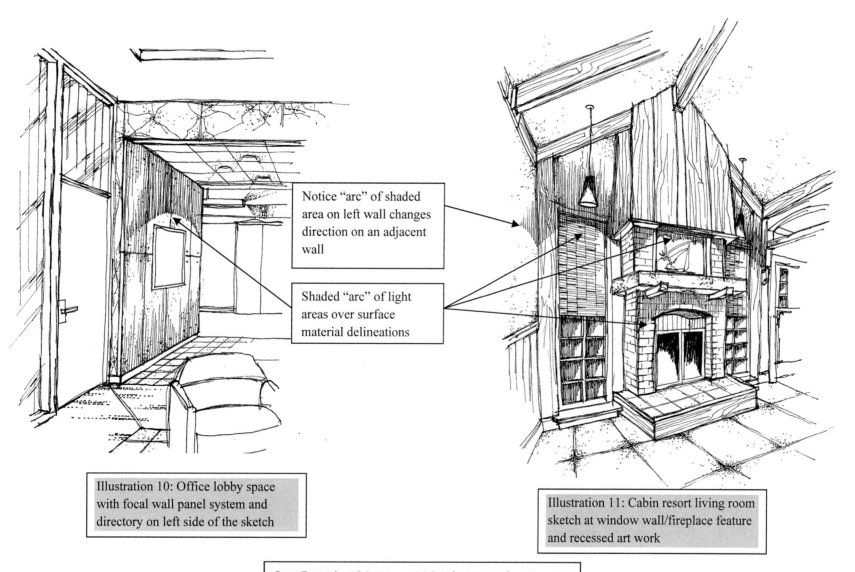

Notice "arc" of shaded area on left wall changes direction on an adjacent wall

Shaded "arc" of light areas over surface material delineations

Illustration 10: Office lobby space with focal wall panel system and directory on left side of the sketch

Illustration 11: Cabin resort living room sketch at window wall/fireplace feature and recessed art work

See Exercise 31, page 146: Ideation Chapter 10

Quick applications of **color** add the sense of realism to the sketch while conveying finish material color, texture, and pattern. If the client or project requires color, the designer should develop a skill level for the application. The color rendering techniques could range from applying color markers, color pencil, watercolor, or a combination of these mediums. The author works primarily with color markers and black felt-tip pens with highlights and shading using color pencil. The more refined/finished felt-tip sketch examples that follow use the *"faded"* color application with a quick stroke technique across the surfaces of features and furnishings. This creates a **brush** effect to the faded strokes.

The natural light source through the left window, on both sketches, is usually drawn with a 45-degree light pencil guideline, even though the path of light during the day is at various angles. Moving further to the right of the room, the natural light source fades, but furnishings and floor surfaces could be highlighted with interior artificial light sources, which these illustrations do not take into account.

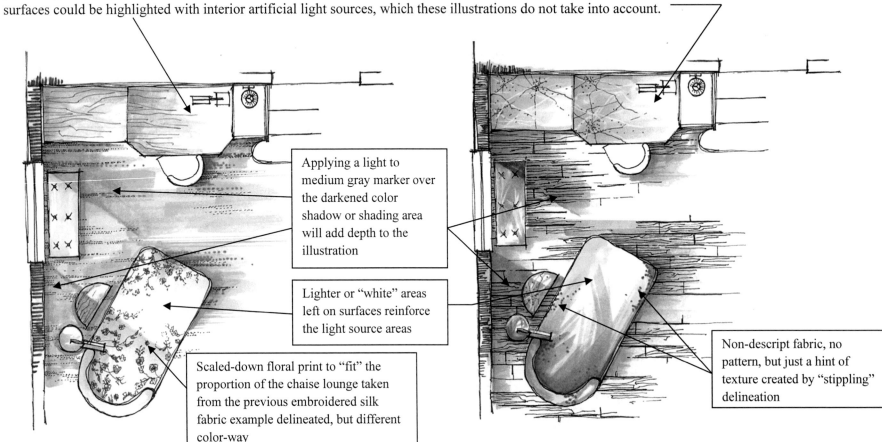

Applying a light to medium gray marker over the darkened color shadow or shading area will add depth to the illustration

Lighter or "white" areas left on surfaces reinforce the light source areas

Scaled-down floral print to "fit" the proportion of the chaise lounge taken from the previous embroidered silk fabric example delineated, but different color-way

Non-descript fabric, no pattern, but just a hint of texture created by "stippling" delineation

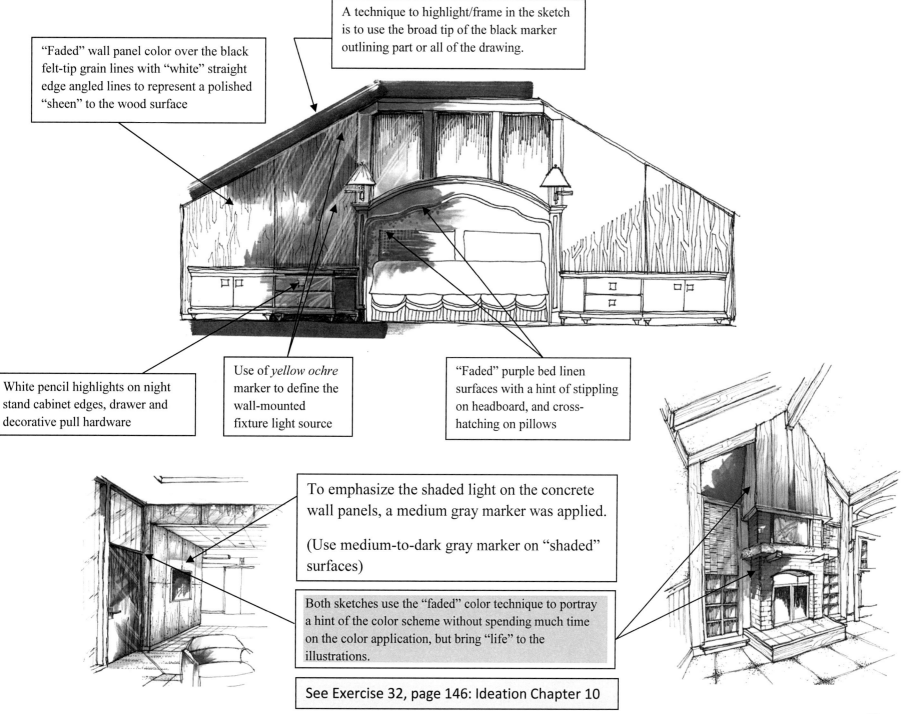

"Faded" wall panel color over the black felt-tip grain lines with "white" straight edge angled lines to represent a polished "sheen" to the wood surface

A technique to highlight/frame in the sketch is to use the broad tip of the black marker outlining part or all of the drawing.

White pencil highlights on night stand cabinet edges, drawer and decorative pull hardware

Use of *yellow ochre* marker to define the wall-mounted fixture light source

"Faded" purple bed linen surfaces with a hint of stippling on headboard, and cross-hatching on pillows

To emphasize the shaded light on the concrete wall panels, a medium gray marker was applied.

(Use medium-to-dark gray marker on "shaded" surfaces)

Both sketches use the "faded" color technique to portray a hint of the color scheme without spending much time on the color application, but bring "life" to the illustrations.

See Exercise 32, page 146: Ideation Chapter 10

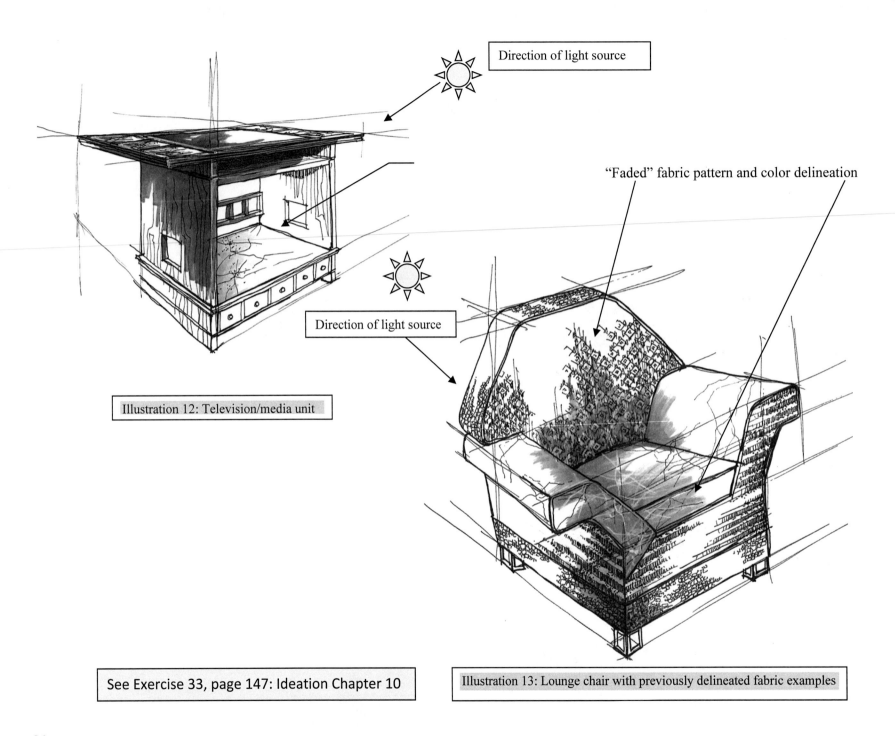

Direction of light source

"Faded" fabric pattern and color delineation

Direction of light source

Illustration 12: Television/media unit

See Exercise 33, page 147: Ideation Chapter 10

Illustration 13: Lounge chair with previously delineated fabric examples

Information and line graphics:

What information is appropriate to convey the illustration?

Font style and sizes

Visual connections and orientation

Color and delineation, why not?

What information is appropriate to convey the illustration?

Even preliminary concept sketches and design development drawings should have reference information to the project and/or client. This could include **"project title"/"client name," drawing "scale," "date" of created sketch, drawing "title," "drawing number or letter," "designer identification," and "north sign"** graphic for any type of **plan.** *An additional crucial* item *of information pertaining to sketched elevations and 3-dimensional illustrations* is the **view or orientation of the sketch.** If any of these items are missing on an illustration, there can be visual misunderstanding and interpretation of the design concept(s). The following illustration examples of the authors' are suggested ways/techniques for conveying information. The designer/student will, through their visual graphic skills, develop a unique "calling-card" graphic depiction of their own. Reflecting back and building on custom block and *architectural* lettering in Ideation Chapter 3 will enhance the designer's ***"information graphics"*** for sketched illustrations.

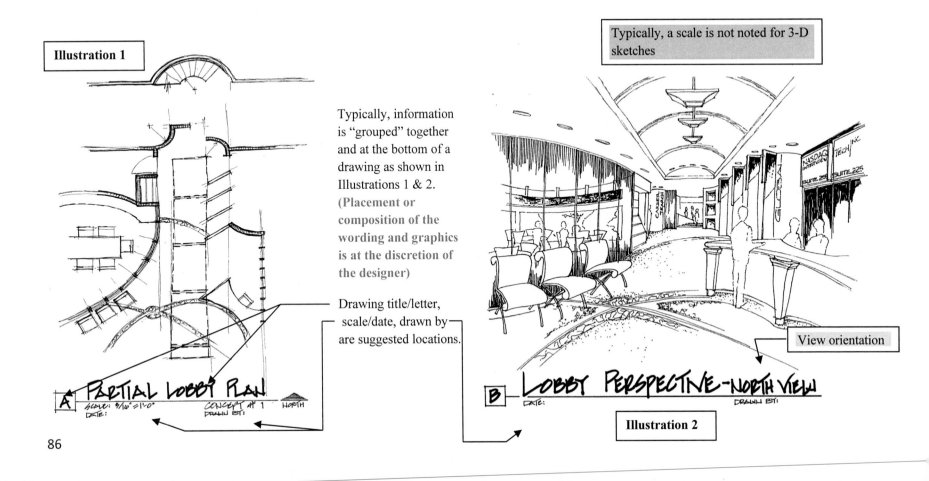

Illustration 1

Typically, a scale is not noted for 3-D sketches

Typically, information is "grouped" together and at the bottom of a drawing as shown in Illustrations 1 & 2. (Placement or composition of the wording and graphics is at the discretion of the designer)

Drawing title/letter, scale/date, drawn by are suggested locations.

View orientation

A PARTIAL LOBBY PLAN
SCALE: 3/16"=1'-0"   CONCEPT # 1   NORTH
DATE: DRAWN BY:

B LOBBY PERSPECTIVE - NORTH VIEW
DATE: DRAWN BY:

Illustration 2

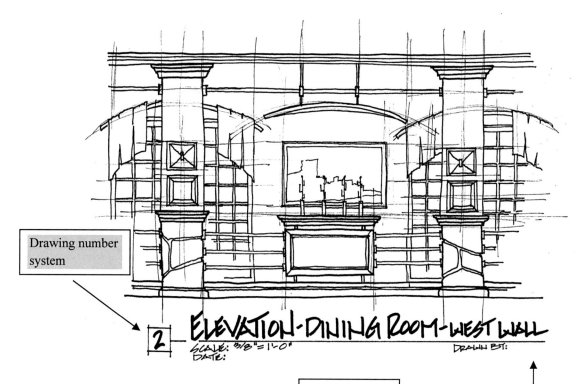

The labeling of the drawing "sequence" can typically be designated as a **letter or number,** but the designer should be consistent in the use of either one for the project or series of hand-sketches. *Stay with a "letter" or "number" system.*

Drawing number system

ELEVATION·DINING ROOM·WEST WALL

Illustration 3

Depicted in Illustrations 1, 2 and 3, what is sometimes called a ***line graphic*** is drawn under the drawing title for a visual composition and communication "system" of the written information. The line graphic obviously draws attention to and adds a visual focus for the drawing.

In free-hand sketching, the font style is either standard *architectural lettering or custom lettering.* Some designers and students of design are highly skilled at creating both types, but if one is learning and practicing the skill, it is a good idea to always use a series light guidelines for consistent lettering height as discussed back in Ideation Chapter 3. Review of the illustrations for font styles and sizes in Chapter 3 would assist in creating your style of free-hand lettering skills. As design student or designer has been trained in architectural or custom lettering techniques, one does develop their unique style of graphic communication for written information.

The designer just needs to be careful in how detailed or delineated the drawing information is to be conveyed, as to not be too visually overwhelming taking away the importance of the sketch itself. The opinion and experience of the author is that a combination of architectural and custom lettering has been well perceived in visually documenting the written information. These types of lettering skills help to emphasize and promote the overall visual look of "hand-sketched" techniques. How much or how little of custom lettering and line graphics to include depends on the type of project and/or amount of visual complexity that the sketch already conveys.

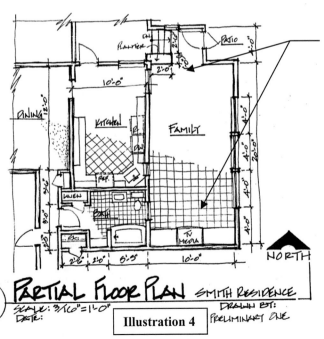

Illustration 4 has a significant amount of space planning information, floor delineations, room titles, dimensions, so a simple architectural lettering style was used. Illustration 5 sketch is not as visually complex, but has a creative space plan movement that custom lettering and delineated graphics could be appropriate to compose.

Illustration 4

Illustration 5

Font size hierarchy suggestions:

Information	Height Size	Line weight	Architectural lettering	Custom lettering
Sketch title	½" to ¾"	Heavy	Solid delineation	Various delineation
Sketch number or letter	½" to ¾"	Heavy	Solid delineation	Various delineation
Client/project title	1/8" to ¾"	Medium	Solid delineation	Solid/various delineation
Scale	1/8" to 3/16"	Medium	Solid delineation	Solid/various delineation
Date	1/8" to 3/16"	Medium	Solid delineation	Solid/various delineation
Drawn By	1/8" to 3/16"	Medium	Solid delineation	Solid/various delineation
Actual information in spaces for Scale, Date, and Drawn By	1/8" to 3/16"	Light to Medium	Solid delineation	
North sign graphic	Varied ½" to ¾"	Heavy		Solid/various delineation
Word "North"	1/8" to ¼"	Heavy	Solid delineation	Solid/various delineation

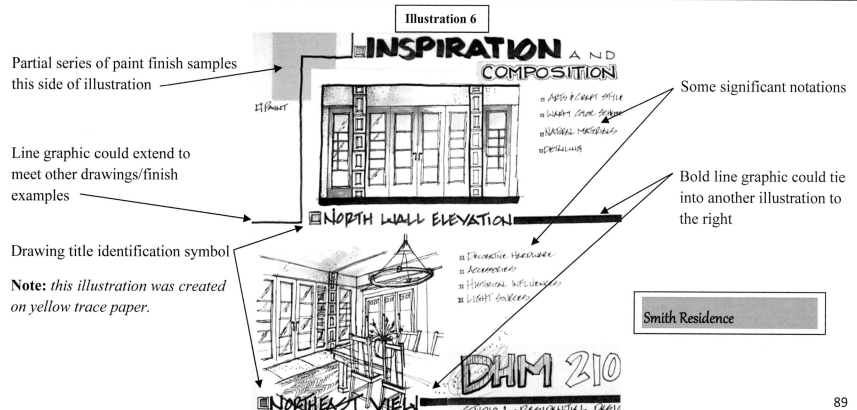

Illustration 6

Partial series of paint finish samples this side of illustration

Line graphic could extend to meet other drawings/finish examples

Drawing title identification symbol

Note: *this illustration was created on yellow trace paper.*

Some significant notations

Bold line graphic could tie into another illustration to the right

Smith Residence

89

Visual connections and orientations

Possible illustration composition layouts for a presentation need to be well thought out. The designer may want to sketch layout compositions on paper first to visualize the "organizational flow" of the illustrations with appropriate ideas for spacing between illustrations, allotment space for the various titles (drawing, project, and sub-titles) and their sizes. Additional thought should be addressed in determining "drawing title identification symbols" as indicated on the previous page, Illustration 6, then the *line graphics* to be incorporated to visually unify the composition ***connectivity.*** This visual composition thought process is also referred to as "story-boarding."

Some designers prefer not to include line graphics and visual connections on their composition presentations; again, these graphic suggestions in this publication are to help convey the design concept if one wishes or thinks "graphics" will aide in the presentation understanding. "Illustration 7" uses a horizontal format composition that could be either on trace or bond paper, while "Illustration 8" could be a vertical format with drawing sketches on a presentation board indicated by the black outline.

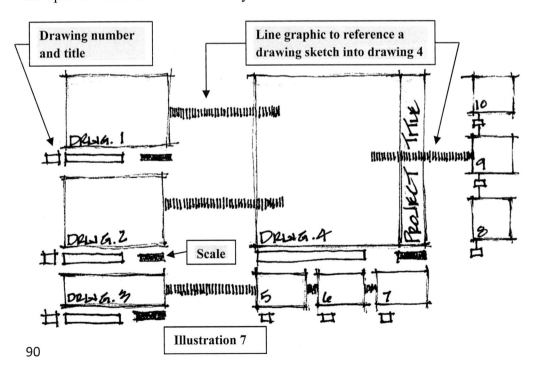

Drawing number and title

Line graphic to reference a drawing sketch into drawing 4

Scale

Illustration 7

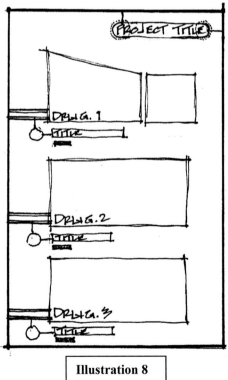

Illustration 8

90

The composition variations are endless, one must just decide on format orientation, scale of all sketches, titles, and appropriate spacing of the presentation elements and graphics. Illustration 9 is the initial story-boarding layout for the final presentation format below in Illustration 10.

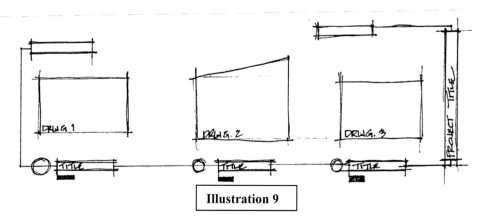

Illustration 9

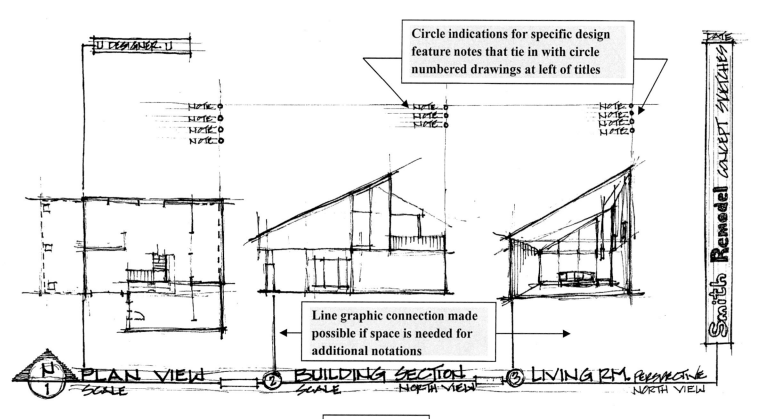

Circle indications for specific design feature notes that tie in with circle numbered drawings at left of titles

Line graphic connection made possible if space is needed for additional notations

Illustration 10

Subtle color and/or delineation techniques can enhance the presentation quality visually drawing attention to the project and title information, but the designer must decide on **how much** or **how little** amount should be indicated. This determination stems from not only design studio experience and individual graphic style, but also, knowing the project intent (image/mood/style), the client (if any) and their perception of color use, and how much detail is incorporated with the sketch already. Usually, designers will add some color and/or delineations for hand-sketched presentation drawings and concept presentations to hopefully gain visual excitement for the project concept and importance to the viewer/audience.

■Illustration 11 below obviously draws attention to the drawing through the use of the color **red** with some stippling delineation in **purple**.

■Illustration 12 below indicates more color since the drawing is somewhat less detailed than *Illustration 11*. The numbered circle and title lettering has a little deeper-to-lighter color hue shading from the bottom of the elements to direct attention upward toward the drawing.

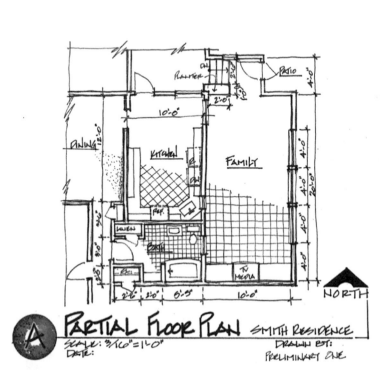

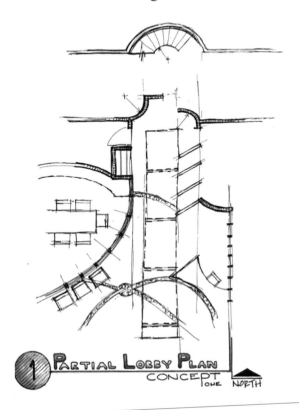

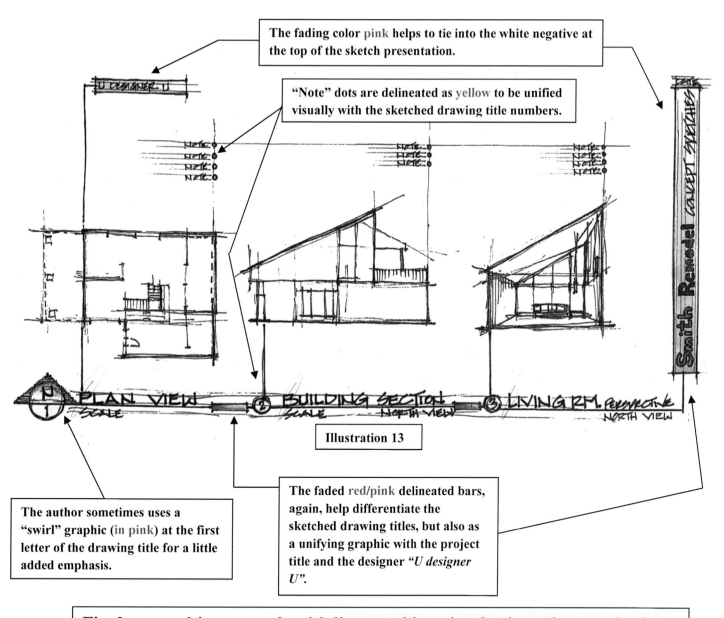

The fading color pink helps to tie into the white negative at the top of the sketch presentation.

"Note" dots are delineated as yellow to be unified visually with the sketched drawing title numbers.

Illustration 13

The author sometimes uses a "swirl" graphic (in pink) at the first letter of the drawing title for a little added emphasis.

The faded red/pink delineated bars, again, help differentiate the sketched drawing titles, but also as a unifying graphic with the project title and the designer "U designer U".

Final composition example with line graphics, visual orientations, and color

See Exercise 34, page 147: Ideation Chapter 10, **"the visual composition"**

When is enough, enough?

*A decision making process for the amount of detail
to incorporate into the visual enhancement of hand-sketched
concept and design development illustrations.*

The author's intent with this short chapter is to offer suggestions to help the designer and design student decide on the level of enhancement to illustrate in concept and design development hand-sketching. After a substantial amount of practicum experience within industry and teaching interior design course work, the author developed a protocol in the decision making process for how much is enough to visually illustrate in a sketch. This shared information is by no means an ultimate way to approach this decision, because one will develop their determining factors, but hopefully, a helpful start.

Think about these factors prior to the level of presentation decision making for the sketch:

1 Have a good understanding of the project scope, intent, and the style/image to be conveyed.

2 Know the presentation reviewer: ***the designer needs to have some psychological insight to the reviewer's thinking and ability to understand levels of visual illustration interpretation.*** A wealth of information can be gathered through the initial interview with the intended reviewer. The reviewer can be a client, the course instructor, or design company staff. Sometimes designers and student designers do not ask enough questions to gain this much needed insight for the quick concept viewing and understanding of the presentation sketch.

3 The type of presentation media to use for the hand-sketched illustration(s). Ideation Chapter 9 will share sketching medium resources.

4 How many illustration sketches/types of sketches are necessary to convey the presentation intent?

5 The appropriate size/scale of the sketch(s).

6 The reviewer's sense and ***appreciation*** of the art of the hand-sketched creative process.

A graphic illustration for the protocol of hand-sketching decision making for the level or visual complexity could be depicted in chart form beginning with simple line drawing sketch compositions to highly visual enhancement detailing as follows:

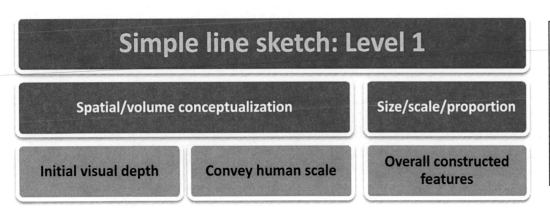

■Ask yourself: *is the sketch to primarily illustrate human scale in relationship to the volume of space and constructed features only?* Then, just a varied line weight sketch is necessary without addressing light sources, furnishings, and material surfacing delineation, as well as color.

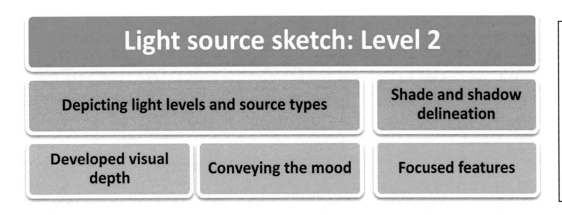

■Ask yourself: *is the sketch to illustrate possible natural and artificial light sources to define feature shapes and enhanced visual depth, creating a particular habitable "mood?"* Then, a more developed sketch is necessary using "generic" shade and shadow delineations, such as stippling and line, or pencil shading techniques.

Furnishings and finishes: Level 3

Depicting concept style/image of the space

Developed interior architectural feature detailing

Indicating furnishings and surface materials

Using delineations to convey particular patterns/textures

Illustrating visual understanding and developed complexity

■Ask yourself: *is the sketch to illustrate specific feature components within the space, such as furnishings, finish materials, constructed features conveying a more developed "mood"/"aesthetic" for the reviewer?* Then, the use of more realistic delineations to depict the suggested pattern/texture selection and light sources is necessary.

Color: Level 4

Color scheme clarification

Enhancement of the concept style/image/mood

Developed shades/shadows/lighting

Developed furnishings and finish material indications

Use of developed color and delineation techniques

Ideation Chapter 8: *"Portfolio of drawing applications"* will share sketch examples illustrating the various levels of detail enhancements.

Portfolio of Illustration Applications:

Plans and elevations

Building sections and construction details

Millwork and furnishings

Perspectives

The intent of this chapter is to share, as a resource, visual inspiration for the student designer and practitioner's skill building development for various levels of hand-sketched presentation requirements. Again, one's technique could have a more "loose" or a more "visually refined" appearance, depending on one's skill comfort level.

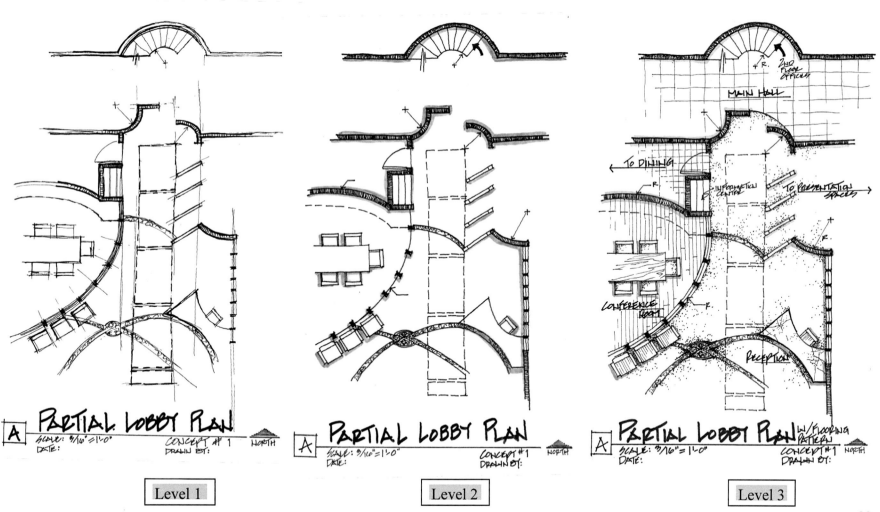

Level 1 | Level 2 | Level 3

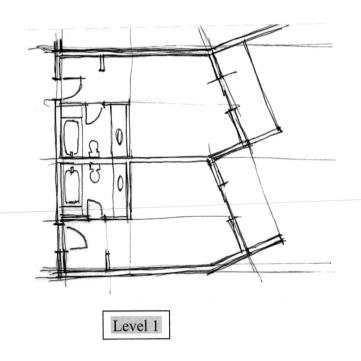

Level 1

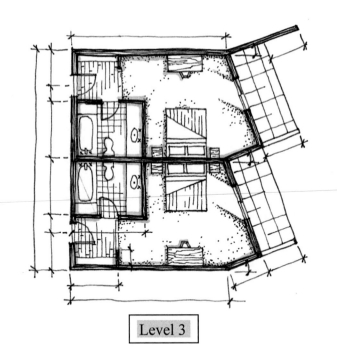

Level 3

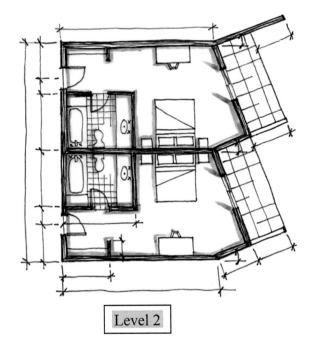

Level 2

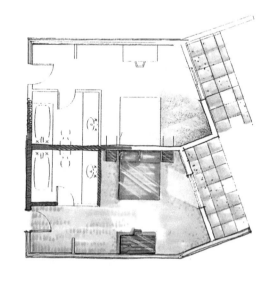

Level 4

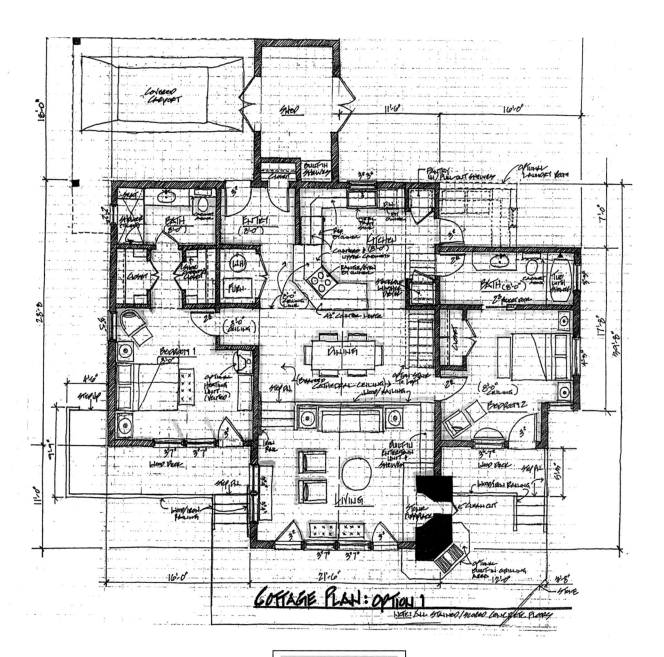

COTTAGE PLAN: OPTION 1

Level 2 or 3 study

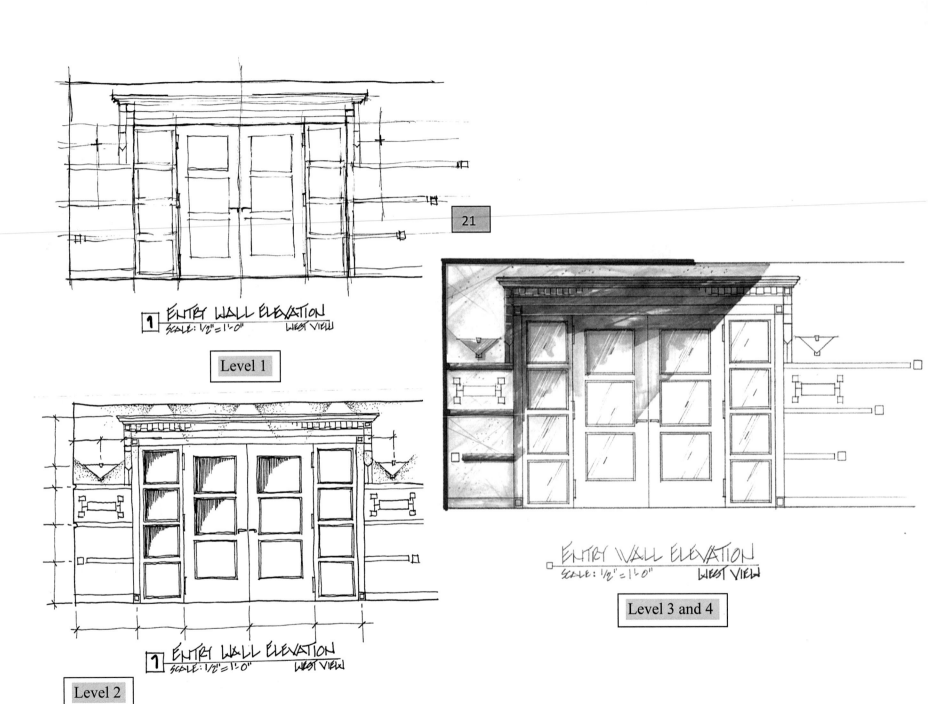

21

ENTRY WALL ELEVATION
1 SCALE: 1/2" = 1'-0"   WEST VIEW

Level 1

ENTRY WALL ELEVATION
1 SCALE: 1/2" = 1'-0"   WEST VIEW

Level 2

ENTRY WALL ELEVATION
SCALE: 1/2" = 1'-0"   WEST VIEW

Level 3 and 4

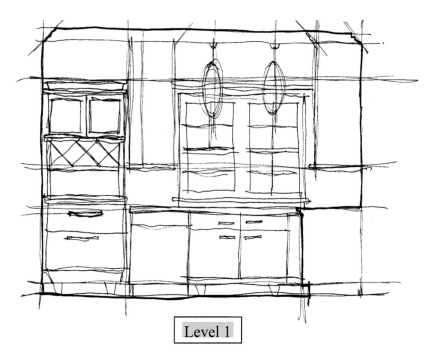

Level 1

Level 3

Level 2

Level 4-modified design

103

Level 3

23

Level 4

Building sections and construction details typically can be illustrated as a Level 1 or 3, since lighting patterns are not depicted.

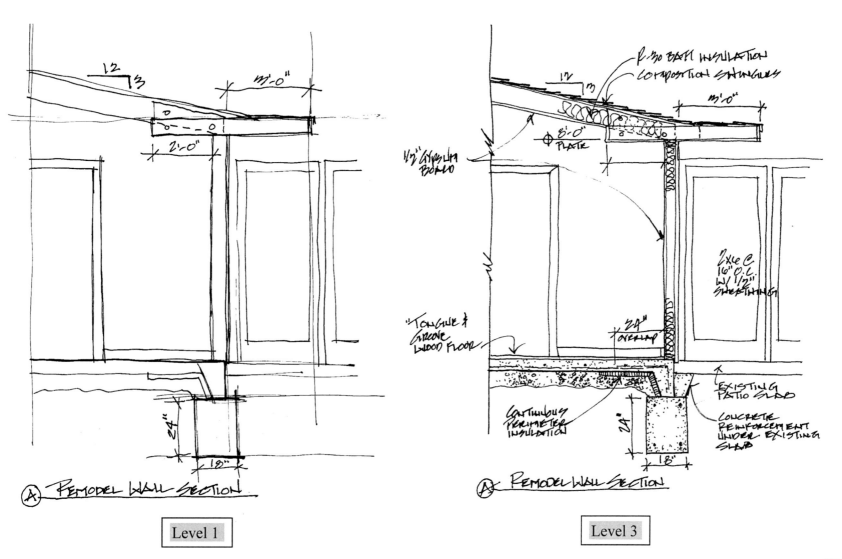

Level 1

Level 3

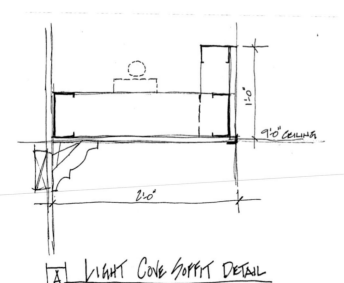

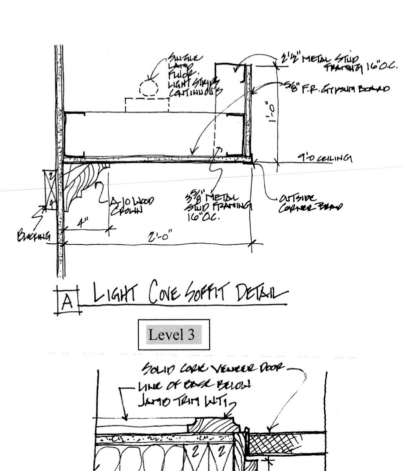

$\boxed{A}$ LIGHT COVE SOFFIT DETAIL

Level 1

$\boxed{A}$ LIGHT COVE SOFFIT DETAIL

Level 3

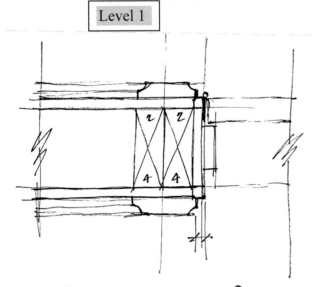

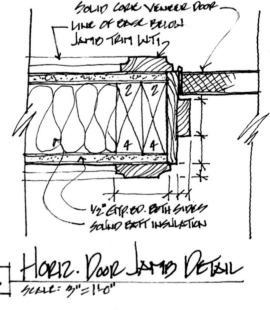

$\boxed{C}$ HORIZ. DOOR JAMB DETAIL
SCALE: 3" = 1'-0"

Level 1

$\boxed{C}$ HORIZ. DOOR JAMB DETAIL
SCALE: 3" = 1'-0"

Level 3

106

Millwork and furnishing details are also typically illustrated as a Level 1 or 3 since lighting issues are not addressed.

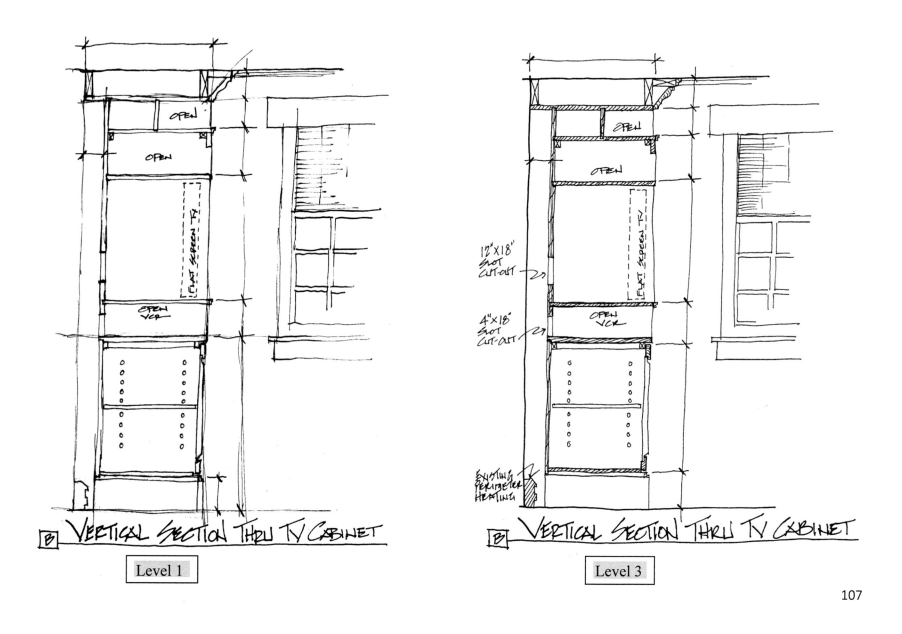

VERTICAL SECTION THRU TV CABINET

Level 1

VERTICAL SECTION THRU TV CABINET

Level 3

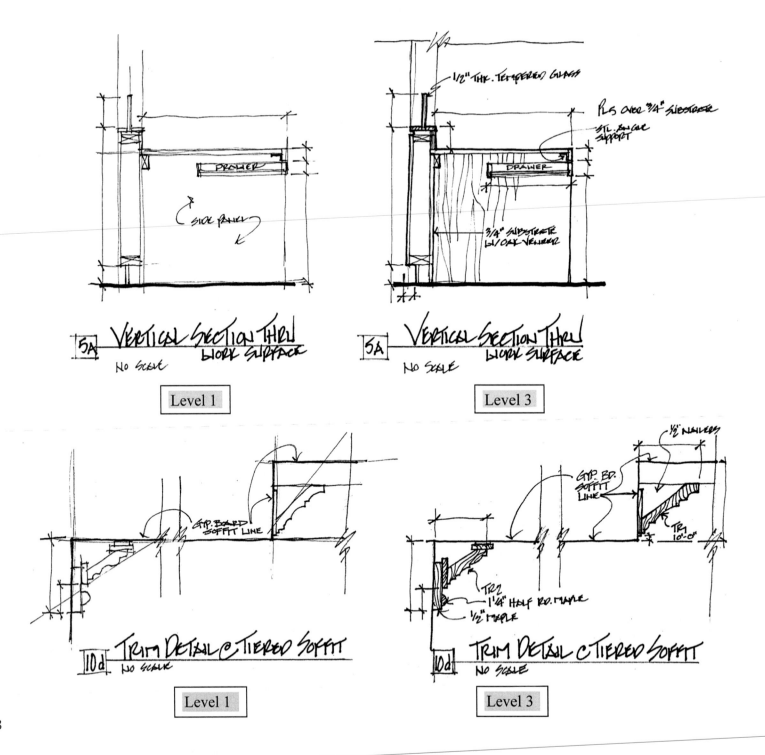

Level 1

Level 3

Level 1

Level 3

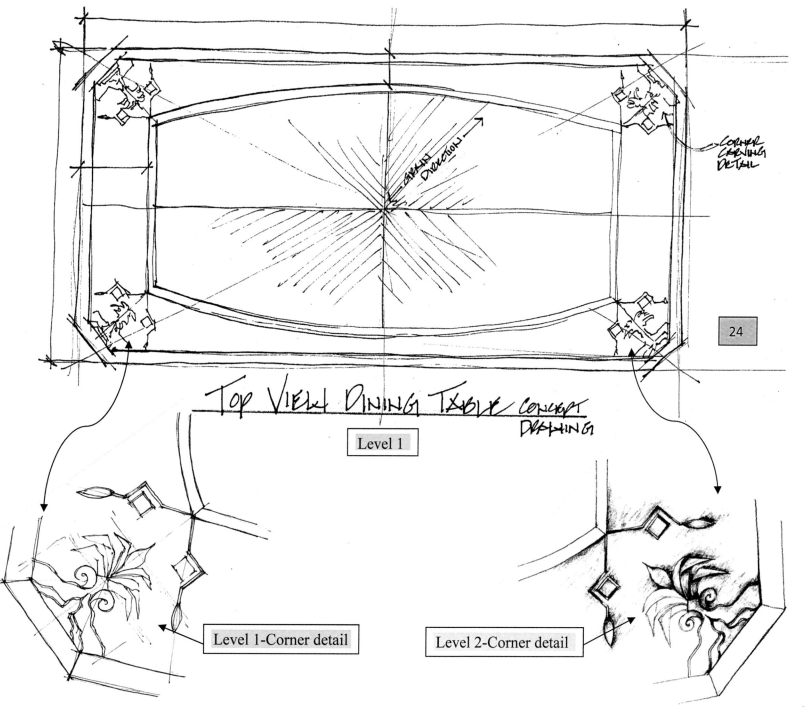

24

CORNER
CARVING
DETAIL

GRAIN DIRECTION →

TOP VIEW DINING TABLE CONCEPT DRAWING

Level 1

Level 1-Corner detail

Level 2-Corner detail

109

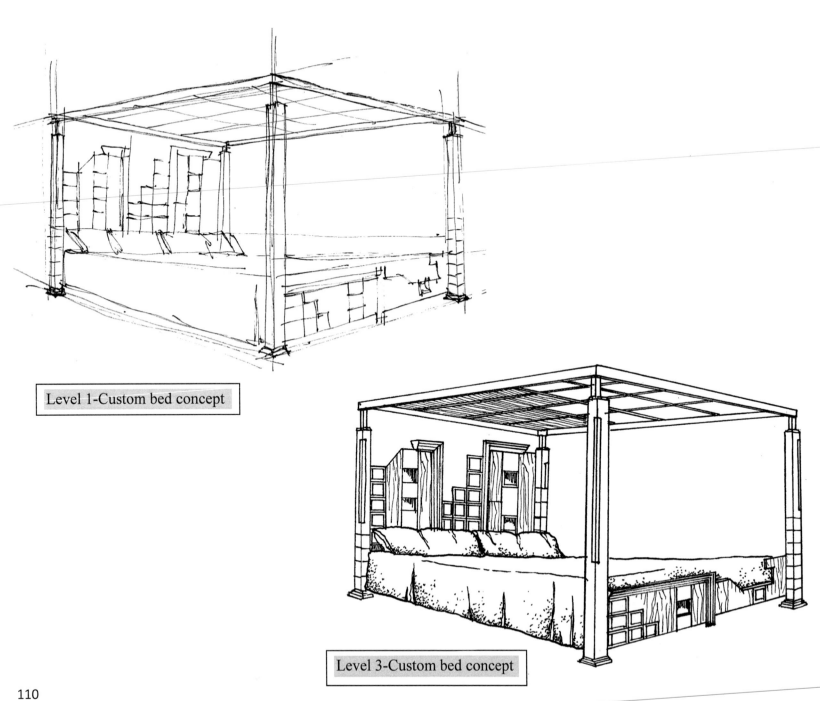

Level 1-Custom bed concept

Level 3-Custom bed concept

110

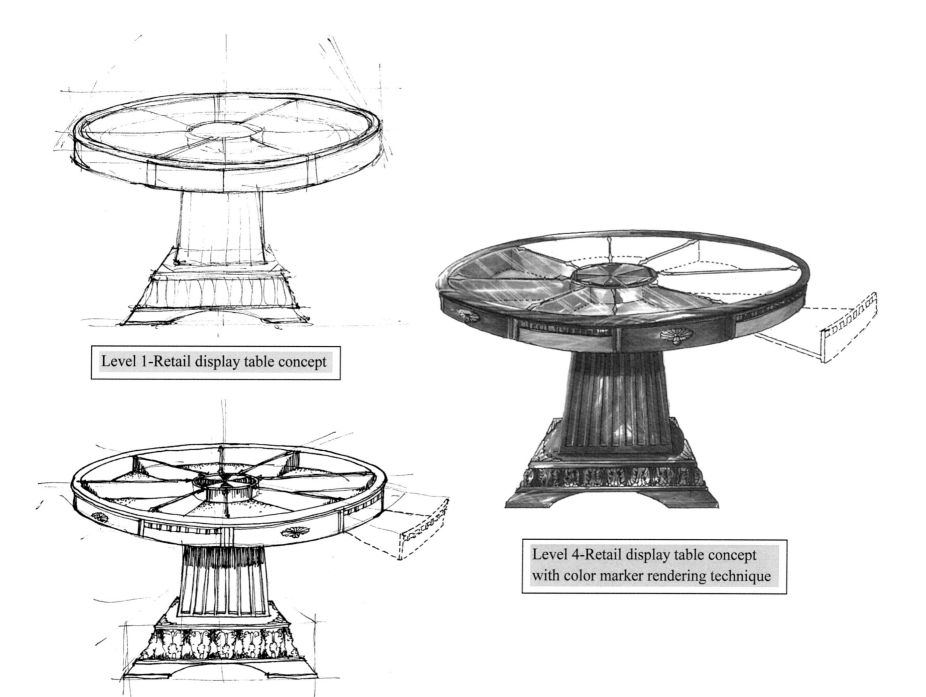

Level 1-Retail display table concept

Level 3-Retail display table concept

Level 4-Retail display table concept
with color marker rendering technique

111

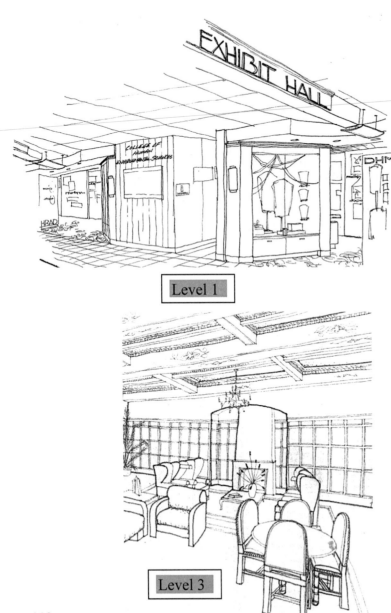

Level 1

Level 2

Level 3

Level 4

Level 1

Level 3-portfolio ready

25

Level 4-portfolio ready

113

Level 1

Level 3-portfolio ready

Level 4-portfolio ready

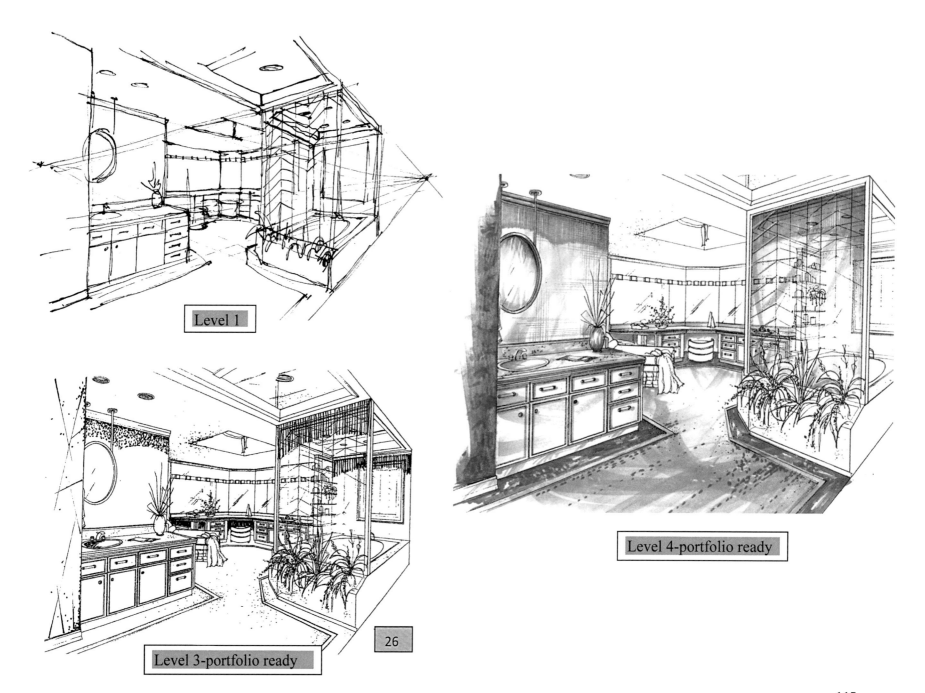

Level 1

Level 3-portfolio ready

26

Level 4-portfolio ready

115

Sketching medium resources

Medium type	Best use with media technique
Trace paper (white or yellow)	Pencil, felt-tip pens, color pencil (result is vivid bold color), and color marker (result is light/transparent color hue)
Blue-line or black-line print	Pencil/color pencil, color marker, felt-tip pens, watercolor, and limited use of pastels
Mylar drafting film	Pencil or "film-o-graph" lead, pen and ink, color pencil (draw on matte side finish for excellent reproduction quality)
"Clear-print" drafting film	Pencil, pen and ink, felt-tip pens, color pencil
"Bond" paper (used in copier machines)	Pencil, felt-tip pens, color pencil, pastels, color marker, and watercolor
Ultra marker paper	Color marker, pastels, pencil and color pencil, pen and ink
"Bienfand" art paper	Watercolor, pastels, pencil and color pencil, pen and ink, charcoal and "Ebony" pencil, felt-tip pens
"Strathmore" color paper (excellent weight and subtle light color background for drawing illustration)	Pencil and color pencil, pastels, pen and ink, color marker, felt-tip, and watercolor
"Strathmore" Bristol board (lightweight but rigid)	Pencil and color pencil, pen and ink, color marker, felt-tip pens, pastel, watercolor, and use for small-scale model mock-ups
"Oak-tag" (light but rigid, inexpensive, and is "buff" in color, great for a background other than "white")	Excellent media choice for color marker, felt-tip pens, pen and ink, pencil and color pencil, pastels, and use for small-scale model mock-ups
"Crescent" Board (fine, texture surface, rigid)	Excellent media choice for watercolor, pen and ink, pencil and color pencil, pastels, limited use with color marker and felt-tip pens due to "bleeding"

Instructions: Based on the 500 square foot space allocation represented by the circle, sketch the proportionate "ratio" circle size next to the square foot amount as indicated.

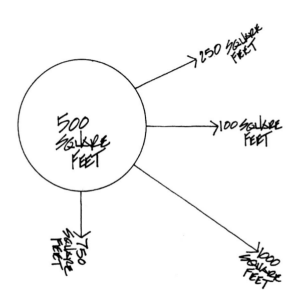

Exercise 1: Bubble Diagramming-
Space allocation proportions

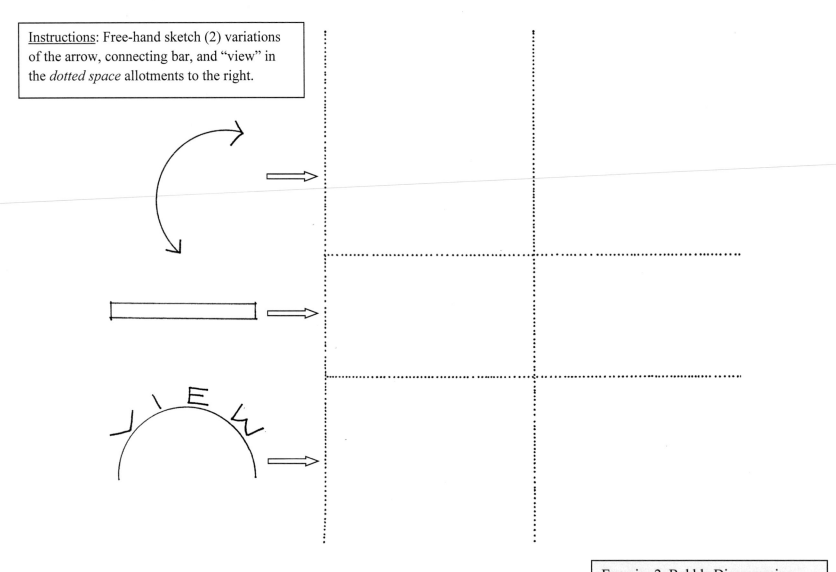

Instructions: Free-hand sketch (2) variations of the arrow, connecting bar, and "view" in the *dotted space* allotments to the right.

Exercise 2: Bubble Diagramming-
Circulation pattern and area
relationship graphics

118

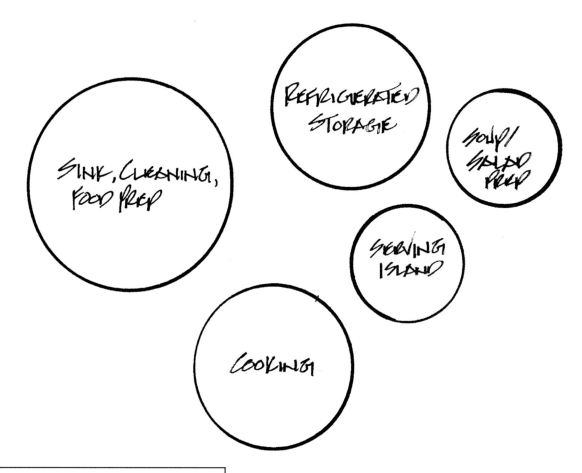

The bubbles in the diagram are labeled:
- SINK, CLEANING, FOOD PREP
- REFRIGERATED STORAGE
- SOUP/ SALAD PREP
- SERVING ISLAND
- COOKING

Instructions: Using symbol "*graphics*," create appropriate primary and secondary circulation pattern identifications for the kitchen bubble diagram. Include "view" graphics and enhance the illustration with black felt-tip delineation techniques.

Exercise 3: Bubble diagram

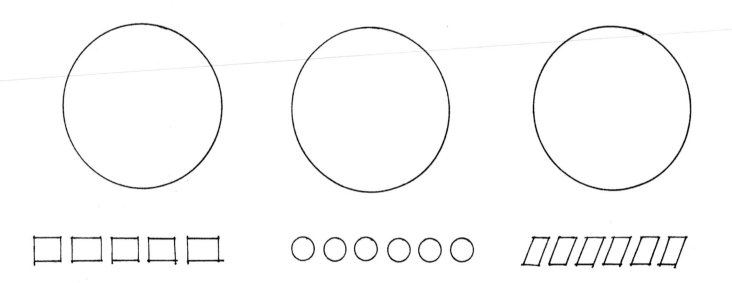

Instructions: Using black felt-tip pens delineate various techniques for the "bubbles" and "connector bars" to enhance the graphic symbols visually.

Exercise 4: Delineation enhancement of the bubble diagramming graphic symbols

HAND-SKETCH

KITCHEN

BUBBLE DIAGRAM

KITCHEN

BUBBLE DIAGRAM

BUBBLE DIAGRAM

Instructions: Using trace paper overlays, create a variety of custom lettering for each line of words provided. Or hand-letter other word titles of your choice.

Experiment with various types of delineations using only black felt-tips.

Exercise 5: Custom lettering

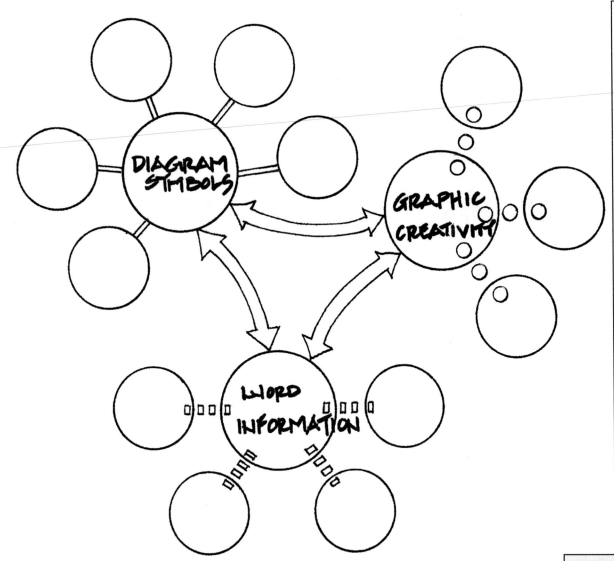

122

Instructions: 1) Hand-letter titles for the blank circles as listed:

"Diagram Symbols"
- space allocations
- views
- adjacencies
- circulation patterns
- special features

"Word Information"
- project information
- notes
- symbol legend
- space identification

"Graphic Creativity"
- line graphics
- color
- delineations

2) Add black felt-tip and color delineation techniques for visual enhancements.

3) Create an illustration title using custom lettering techniques

Exercise 6: Bubble diagram enhancements

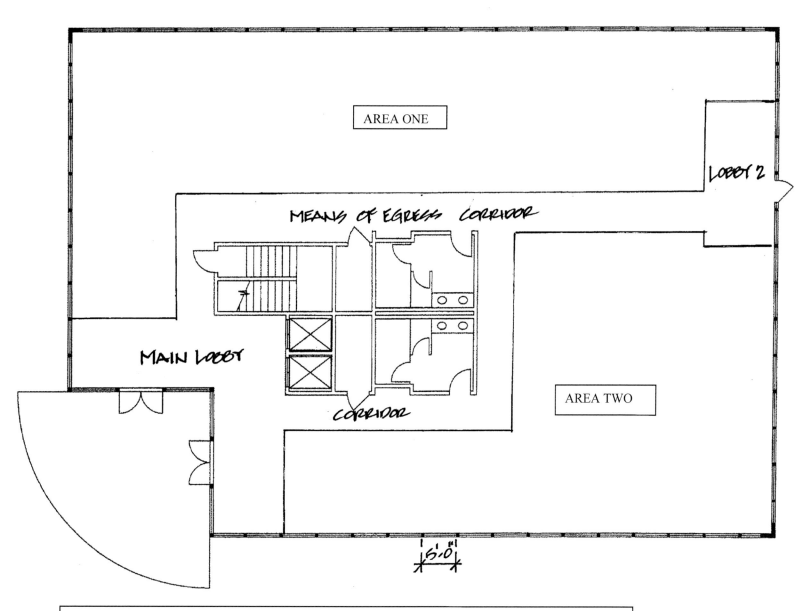

AREA ONE

LOBBY 2

MEANS OF EGRESS CORRIDOR

MAIN LOBBY

CORRIDOR

AREA TWO

5'-0"

Instructions: Create a space block plan for (2) small business offices in "AREA ONE" and (1) business office in "AREA TWO." Then, enhance the illustration to clearly identify "means of egress," the three office area components, using delineation and color techniques.

Exercise 7: Space block plans

Exercise 8: Grid-scaling- *creating proportional grid units*

124

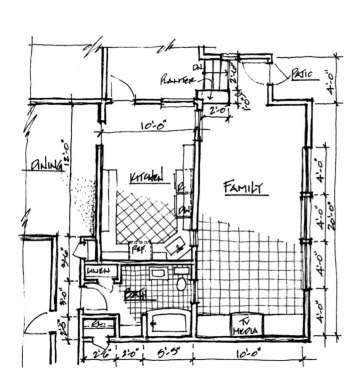

Instructions: Using the grid to represent 2"-0" modules, reproduce the floor plan above with a trace paper overlay.

Exercise 9: Floor plan "grid scaling"

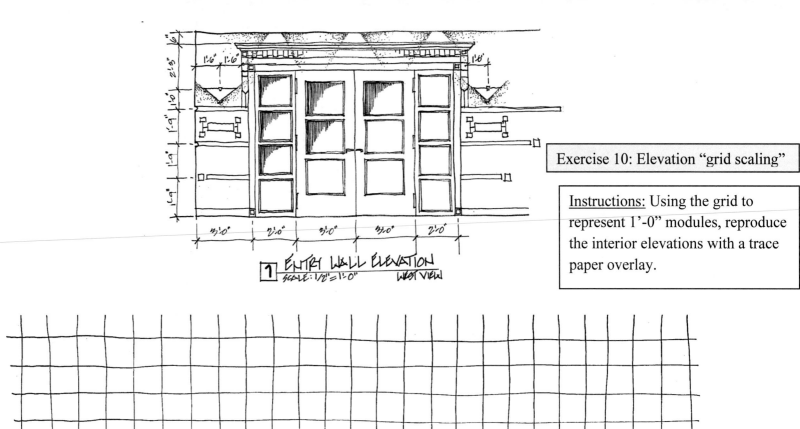

1 ENTRY WALL ELEVATION
SCALE: 1/2"=1'-0"   WEST VIEW

Exercise 10: Elevation "grid scaling"

Instructions: Using the grid to represent 1'-0" modules, reproduce the interior elevations with a trace paper overlay.

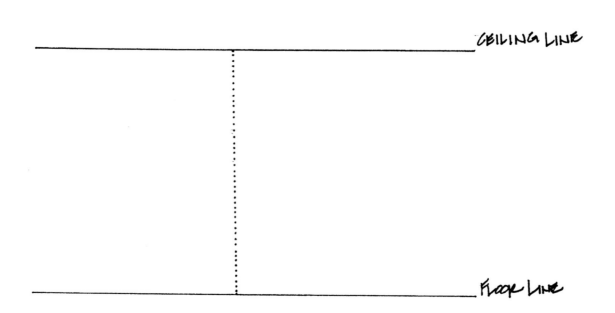

CEILING LINE

FLOOR LINE

Exercise 11: One-point perspective-
line rough layout

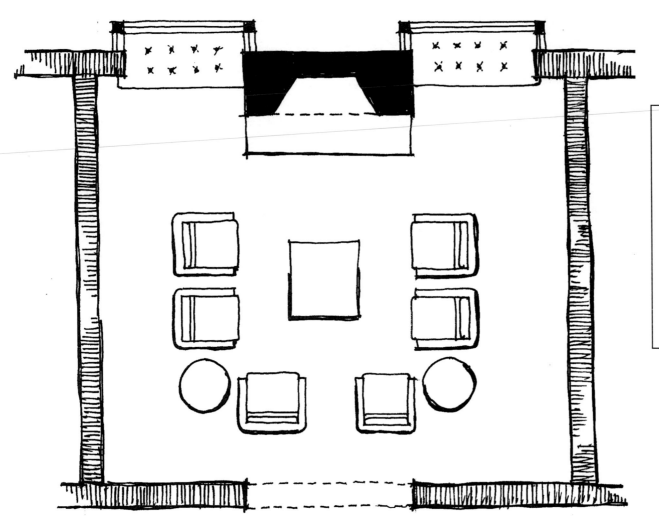

Instructions: Create a one-point perspective of the formal living room floor plan drawn at ¼" = 1'-0" scale using the "grid" method of illustration.

Include the furnishings and window sill, window height, and fireplace features sizing are at the discretion of the designer.

Exercise 12: One-point perspective

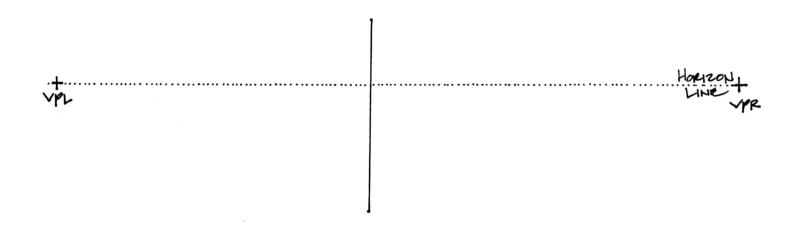

VPL

HORIZON LINE

VPR

Exercise 13: Two-point perspective-
line rough layout

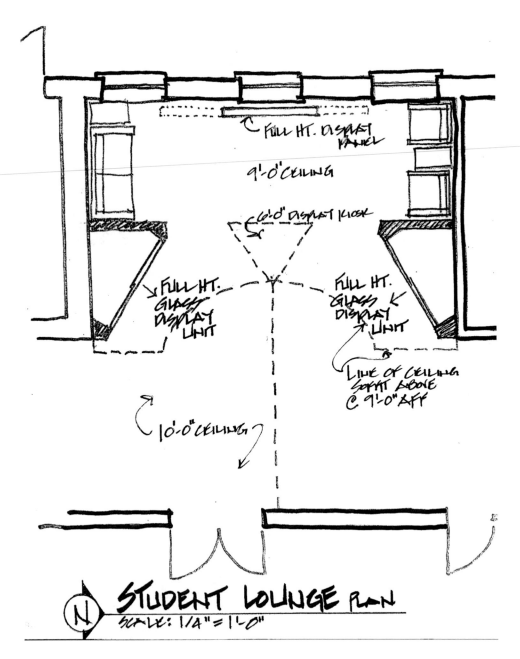

FULL HT. DISPLAY PANEL

9'-0" CEILING

6'-0" DISPLAY KIOSK

FULL HT. GLASS DISPLAY UNIT

FULL HT. GLASS DISPLAY UNIT

LINE OF CEILING SOFFIT ABOVE @ 9'-0" AFF

10'-0" CEILING

STUDENT LOUNGE PLAN
SCALE: 1/4" = 1'-0"

Instructions: Create a two-point perspective of the student lounge plan drawn at ¼" =1'-0" scale.

Window sill and window height are at the discretion of the designer.

Exercise 14: Two-point perspective

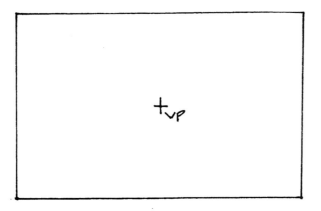

Exercise 15: "Bird's-eye" perspective-
line rough layout

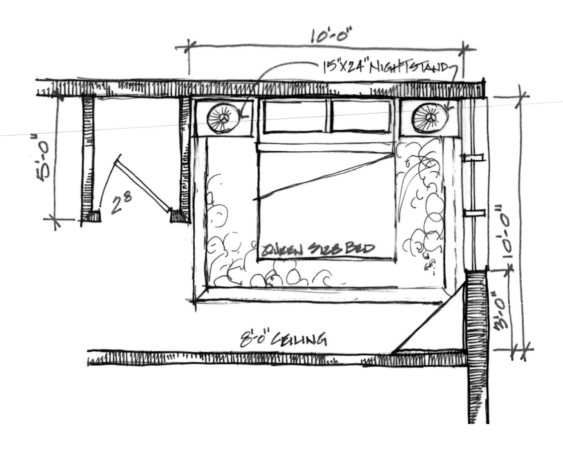

10'-0"

15"X24" NIGHTSTAND

5'-0"

2⁸

10'-0"

3'-0"

QUEEN SIZE BED

8'-0" CEILING

Instructions: Create a "bird's eye" perspective of the bedroom including the furnishings depicted. Window sill and window height is at the discretion of the designer. The width of the closet is 3'-0," interior partitions are 5" thick and exterior walls are 8" thick.

Exercise 16: "Bird's-eye" perspective

← UNIT CORNER LINE

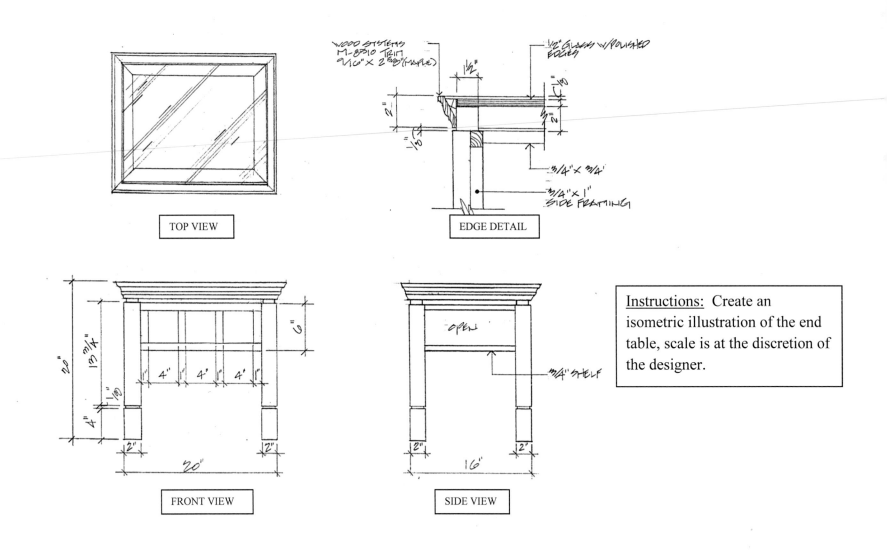

WOOD SYSTEMS
M-8910 TRIM
9/16" X 2 5/8" (MAPLE)

1/2" GLASS W/POLISHED
EDGES

1 1/2"

2"

2"

3/4" X 3/4"

3/4" X 1"
SIDE FRAMING

TOP VIEW

EDGE DETAIL

20"

13 3/4"

6"

1"

4"

1"

4"

1"

4"

1"

4"

OPEN

3/4" SHELF

2"

2"

20"

16"

2"

2"

FRONT VIEW

SIDE VIEW

Instructions: Create an isometric illustration of the end table, scale is at the discretion of the designer.

Exercise 18: Furniture isometric

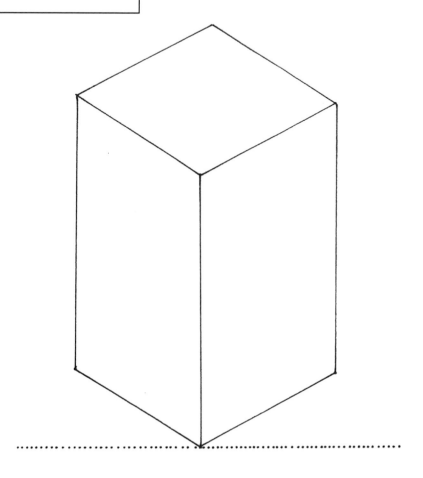

Exercise 19: Upholstered furniture isometric sketch

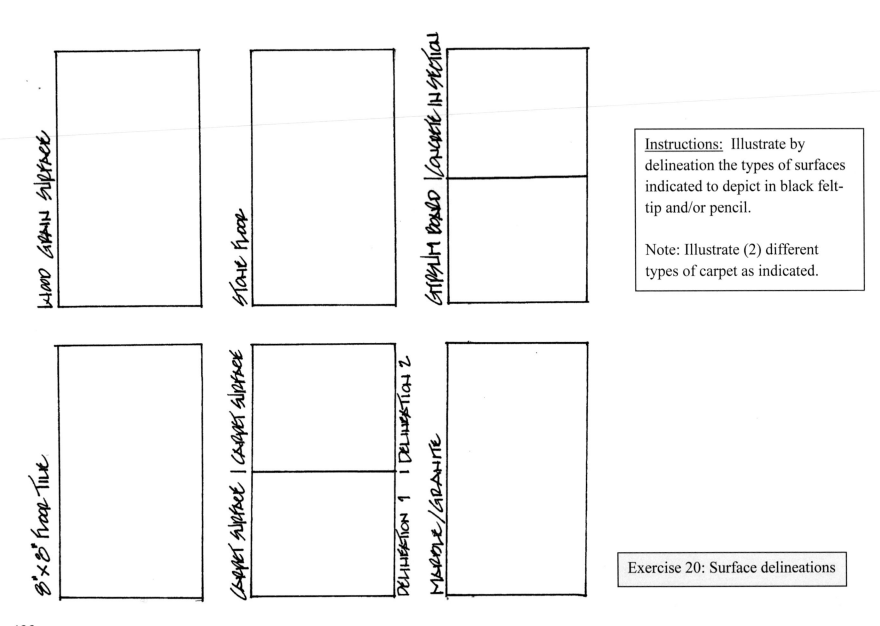

WOOD GRAIN SURFACE

STONE FLOOR

GYPSUM BOARD | CONCRETE IN SECTION

8" x 8" FLOOR TILE

CARPET SURFACE | CARPET SURFACE

DELINEATION 1 | DELINEATION 2

MARBLE / GRANITE

Instructions: Illustrate by delineation the types of surfaces indicated to depict in black felt-tip and/or pencil.

Note: Illustrate (2) different types of carpet as indicated.

Exercise 20: Surface delineations

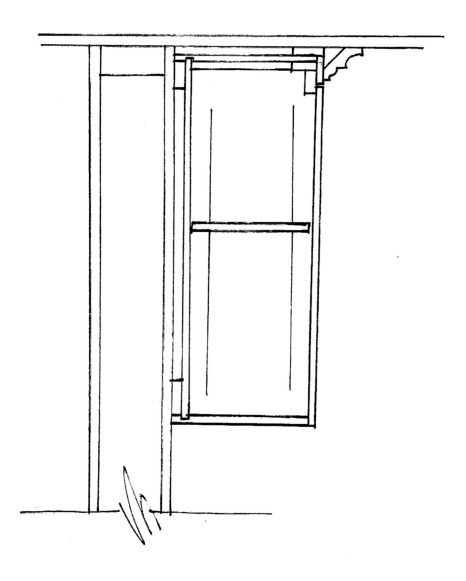

Instructions: Depict the appropriate types of building material delineation for the upper cabinet section attached to a 2 X 4 residential partition construction.

Exercise 21: Materials in section

Instructions: Hand-sketch various trace paper overlay *drapery* window treatments for the window wall below. Experiment with covering the entire glazing area, one-way draw, and two-way draw opening. Add a cornice board or valance treatment. Experiment with a subtle **geometric** fabric pattern as a sketch option.

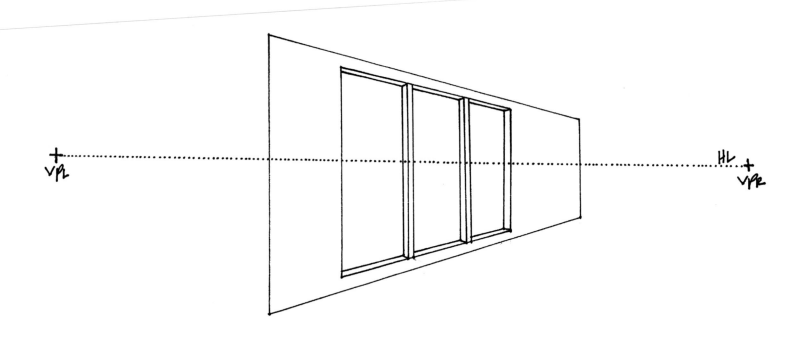

Exercise 22: Window treatment sketching

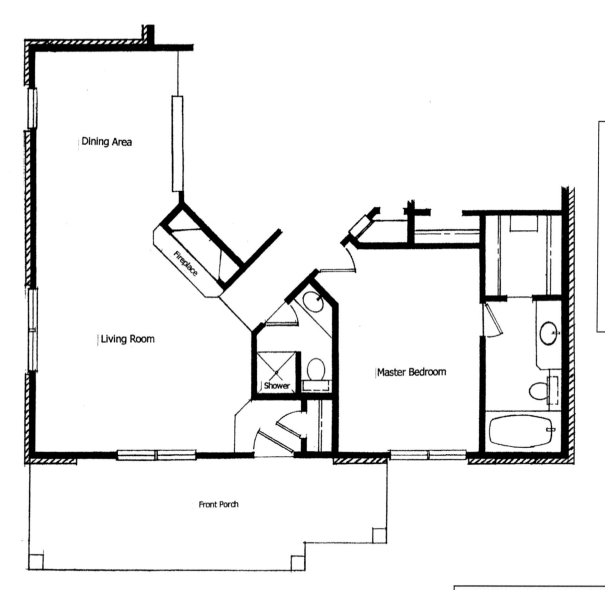

Dining Area

Fireplace

Living Room

Shower

Master Bedroom

Front Porch

Instructions: Using a trace paper overlay of the floor plan drawn at 1/8" = 1'-0" scale, illustrate appropriate furnishings and their sizes for the dining, living, and master bedroom areas.

Then, illustrate floor covering surfaces.

Exercise 23: Floor plan with furnishings and floor types

139

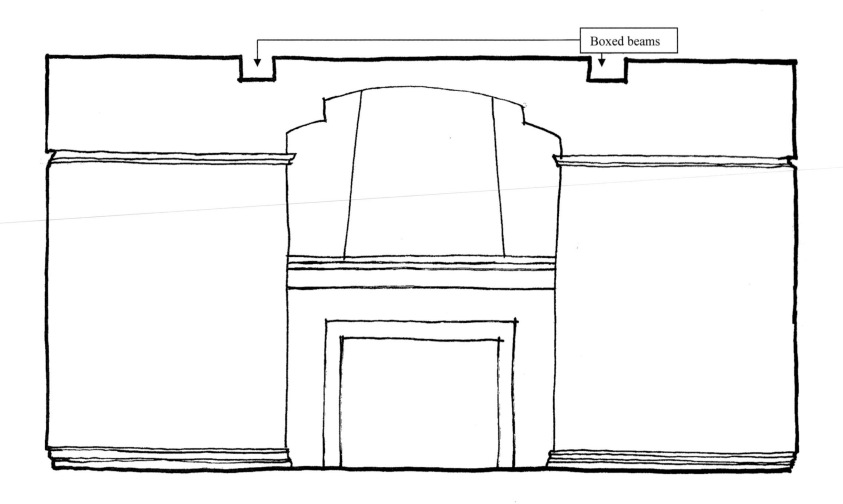

Boxed beams

Instructions: Indicate various finish material surface treatments using delineation techniques either on a copy of this drawing or on a trace overlay.

Exercise 24: Interior wall elevation

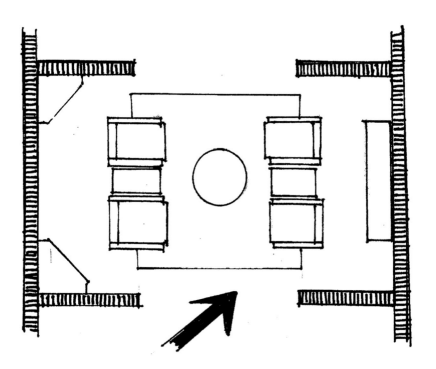

Exercise 25: Two-point perspective-*line rough layout*

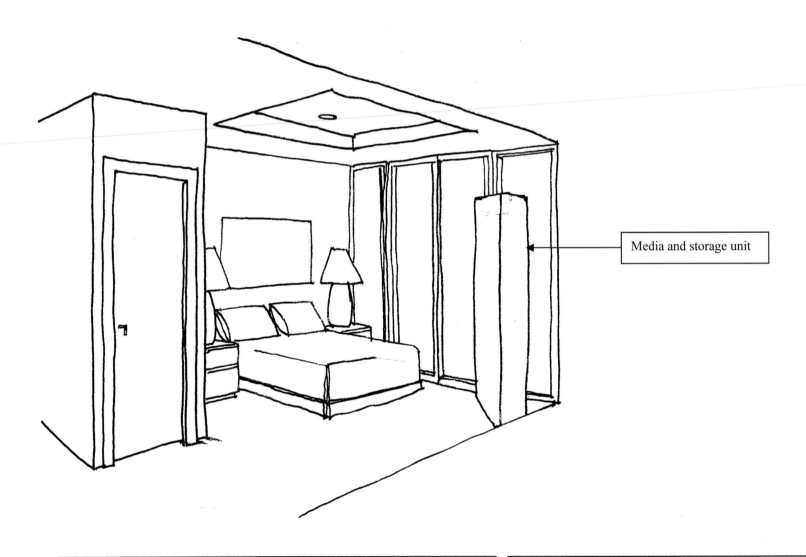

Media and storage unit

Instructions: Indicate finish material delineations on all surfaces and room features/furnishings.

Exercise 26: Two-point bedroom interior perspective

Fabric sample illustration credit: S. Harris/Fabricut-Tulsa,
Oklahoma. Pattern: Bombay, Color: Saffron

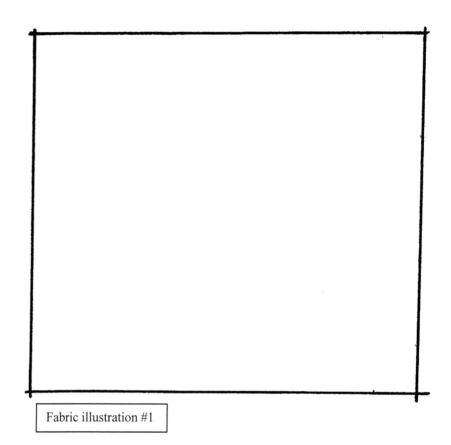

Fabric illustration #1

Fabric illustration #2

Instructions: Using black felt-tip pens, proportionally illustrate the fabric sample
shown to "fit" the entire box for Fabric illustration #1 and #2 to experiment with the
scale of the same pattern.

Exercise 27: Fabric illustration

143

Chair fabric illustration #2

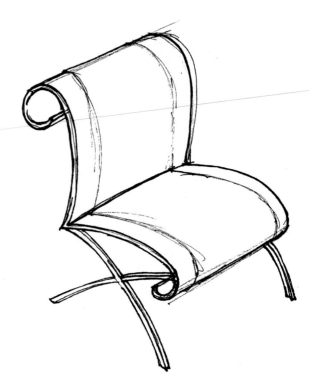

Chair fabric illustration #1

Instructions: Illustrate the fabric sketched on the previous page on Chair fabric illustration #1 and #2 to experiment with various pattern scales. Use black felt-tips on a copy of this drawing or on trace paper overlay.

Exercise 28: Fabric applications

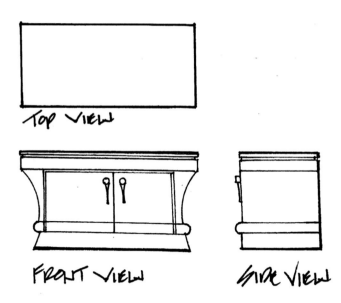

Top View

Front View   Side View

Instructions: Using the line rough furniture views to the left of the storage unit with a pair of doors, create a two-point perspective of the piece, then, delineate finish materials in black felt-tip. The dimensional sizes are at the discretion of the designer.

Exercise 29: Furniture storage unit two-point perspective with finish material delineation technique

145

Exercise 30: Using the finish material surface delineation drawing in "Exercise 24", create a *light source* concept for the elevation sketch.

Exercise 31: Using the finish material surface delineation drawing in "Exercise 26", create a *light source* concept for the perspective sketch.

Exercise 32: Using the light source concept perspective sketch in "Exercise 26", enhance the illustration with a color rendering technique (color markers or color pencils, or a combination of both).

Visual inspiration for Exercises 30, 31, and 32

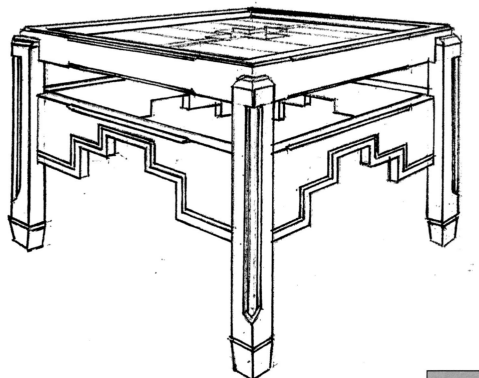

Instructions: Delineate and/or "spot" color render the Southwest occasional table. Copy onto 2-3 types of paper, such as "bond/copy" paper, "oak tag", and "trace" paper overlay, experimenting with a different illustration technique on each medium source.

Exercise 34: Select and photocopy 4-5 of your finished exercises that would complement each other to create a *total visual composition* on an 18" X 24" foam core board. Unify the composition with custom letter graphics (drawing titles, "Composition Title", and line graphics). Selection of foam core board should complement the choice of exercise drawings.

Refer to Ideation Chapter 6: Information and Line Graphics for inspiration.

1-Henk-Seng Design, Tulsa, Oklahoma, sketch for 2011 Tulsa Designer Showcase House, Campbel l Hotel Suite.

2-Kinslow, Keith, and Todd, Inc., Tulsa Oklahoma, sketch for Meridian Tower parking garage entry.

3-September/October 2002 *Home Planning Ideas®,* Photography by Hedrich Blessing Studio. ©2002 Meredith Corporation. Magazine, All rights reserved.

4-June Gilliam, ASID, Stillwater, Oklahoma, sketch for residential client architectural features, Scottsdale, Arizona.

5-Newton Residence, Catoosa, Oklahoma, sketch for floor pattern design.

6-Tony Sabelo, former Oklahoma State University student bubble diagram project, practicing interior designer for SGA Design Group, Tulsa, Oklahoma.

7-David Denham Interiors, Tulsa, Oklahoma, sketch Tulsa Designer Showcase House powder bath.

8-Quida Kelly, Q3, Tulsa, Oklahoma, sketch for Tulsa Designer Showcase House kitchen.

9-June Gilliam, ASID, Stillwater, Oklahoma, sketch for residential client master bedroom, Scottsdale, Arizona.

10-June Gilliam, ASID, Stillwater, Oklahoma, sketch for residential client master bedroom, Scottsdale, Arizona.

11-Lynn Knight Jesse, Kitchen Concepts, Tulsa, Oklahoma, sketch for residential client library.

12-Susie Woody, Woody Designs, Tulsa, Oklahoma, Sandra Sober, Tulsa, Oklahoma, Tamara Logsdon Hawkinson, Writer, Scottsdale, Arizona & Tulsa, Oklahoma, sketch for university library lounge.

13-June Gilliam, ASID, Stillwater, Oklahoma, exterior sketch for personal private residence.

14-June Gilliam, ASID, Stillwater, Oklahoma, exterior elevation sketch for residential developer, Flagstaff, Arizona.

15-June Gilliam, ASID, Stillwater, Oklahoma, sketch for dining table/chair concept for a retail showroom.

16-Kinslow, Keith, and Todd, Inc., Tulsa, Oklahoma, sketch for Copper Oaks office lobby, Tulsa, Oklahoma.

17-Fabricut Showroom, 9303 East 46th St.-Tulsa, Oklahoma, Fabric pattern: Argentina-F, Color: 2.

18-Fabricut Showroom, 9303 East 46th St.-Tulsa, Oklahoma, Fabric pattern: Mynah, Color: 01.

19-Fabricut Showroom, 9303 East 46th St.-Tulsa, Oklahoma, Fabric pattern: Distributors, Color: 01.

20-S. Harris/Fabricut Showroom, 9303 East 46th St.-Tulsa, Oklahoma, Fabric pattern: Sungari,
    Color: Gold

21-Oklahoma State University-Tulsa, sketch for student lounge entry door wall.

22-Mike Raburn, Claremore, Oklahoma and Jay Rambo Company, Tulsa, Oklahoma, sketch for residential
    client kitchen wall concept, Tulsa, Oklahoma.

23-"2012"- Tulsa Designer Showcase House, Tulsa Public School System, exterior sketch.

24-Renee Daugherty and Mark Wakefield Residence, Jenks, Oklahoma, sketch for custom dining
    table top.

25-Charles Faudree Interiors, Tulsa, Oklahoma, sketch for Tulsa Designer Showcase House living room.

26-June Gilliam, ASID, Stillwater, Oklahoma, sketch for residential client master bath.

27-S. Harris/Fabricut Showroom, 9303 East 46th St.-Tulsa, Oklahoma, Fabric pattern: Bombay,
    Color: Saffron.